A Year of Love

Finding peace one day at a time

Courtney Symes

A Little Pink Book Publishing

AUSTRALIA

Copyright © 2021 by Courtney Symes

All rights reserved. No part of this publication may be reproduced, distributed or transmitted in any form or by any means, without prior written permission.

Courtney Symes/A Little Pink Book Publishing
P.O Box 3332
Belconnen, ACT, 2617
www.alittlepinkbook.com

Publisher's Note: Courtney Symes has asserted her right under the Copyright, Designs and Patents Act 1988 to be identified as the author of this work. The information in this book is based on the author's experiences and opinions. The publisher specifically disclaims responsibility for any adverse consequences, which may result from use of the information contained herein. Permission to use information has been sought by the author. Any breaches will be rectified in further editions of the book.

Cover design: Little Miss Prickles
Editor: Shauna Upson
Book Layout © 2021 BookDesignTemplates.com

A Year of Love/ Courtney Symes. -- 1st ed.
ISBN 978-0-6451646-2-6

Dedication:

For my family. You are my greatest loves.

For Hannah. Because you and your little loves were taken away too soon.

Because everyone deserves to love and be loved.

"There is no greater power in the Universe than the power of love. The feeling of love is the highest frequency you can emit. If you could wrap every thought in love, if you could love everything and everyone, your life would be transformed."

— RHONDA BYRNE, THE SECRET

Contents

Preface 6

The Journey Begins 1

The Art of Self-Love... 7

Love the Skin You're In.. 27

Love What You Do 69

Family: Where Life Begins and Love Never Ends
.... 107

Friends Are the Family We Choose................... 157

Friends with Fur, Wings, and Other Things 167

Home is Where the Heart Is 191

The Natural World 215

The Power Within 259

The Journey Continues ….................................. 293

Preface

My *Year of Love* took place in 2019, in the time before COVID-19 wreaked havoc on our world and prior to the catastrophic bushfires that devastated many parts of Australia.

Over the last two years, our world has endured the loss of homes, livelihoods, and life from bushfires and the pandemic. The crippling impact of COVID-19 has also rippled through every economy.

Even though this book was lovingly written before these unprecedented events, the insights and messages on the following pages mean *more than ever.* We have never needed love more than we do now – love for each other, love for ourselves, and love for our planet.

The future remains uncertain, but I hope with all my heart it is one filled with love – for us and our world.

• CHAPTER 1 •

The Journey Begins

Who is this book for?

This book is written as a gift of love to anyone who feels restless, lost, confused, scared, or uncertain about the path they are travelling on through life. This book is for anyone who has ever thought they are not *enough* for their family, friends, work, society, or most importantly, themselves.

This is a book about love - in all its magnificent capacities - but most importantly, about the love we have for ourselves. Without self-love, we impact our ability to love anyone or anything purely and unconditionally.

This book shares some simple truths:
1. Love is at the heart of everything.
2. Love is free.
3. We can choose to return to love at any time – regardless of what else is going on around us.

Why Love

My life isn't, nor will it ever be, 'perfect'. We are *all* imperfectly perfect. But life can be better. Everyone can absolutely make the most of what they already have – especially when they see it through a lens of love. The difference between settling with where you're at or choosing to maximise your current resources is where *the magic* happens.

Before embarking on this journey, my days were busy. Each waking moment was filled with work, family, friends, housework, etc. If you asked me how I was, I'd reply, "really busy!" Busyness had become my new form of procrastination and the reason I hadn't moved the needle towards most of my big-ticket goals. Suddenly, both my children were in primary school and were learning to read, could dress themselves, and thought Peppa Pig was for 'babies' ... and I was left wondering where the last seven years of my life went. While there was nothing fundamentally wrong with my life, deep down, I knew I wasn't reaching my potential or connecting with my higher self.

In her book, *The Happiness Project: Or Why I Spent a Year Trying to Sing in the Morning, Clean My Closets, Fight Right, Read Aristotle, and Generally Have More Fun*, Gretchen Rubin remarks, "I don't want to reject my life. I want to change my life without changing my life", which is exactly where I was at when I embarked on this journey. This is the book I needed to read, so this is the book I have written for myself. It is the greatest gift I could give myself. My wish is for this book to touch and inspire others in the same way it made me feel when writing it.

I have long suspected that 'love' – in all its many shapes and forms, is the sole purpose of our existence. I have encountered this concept in numerous books from authors such as Neale Donald Walsch, Marianne Williamson, Matt Kahn, et al.

Eben Alexander M.D. provides a beautiful explanation of love in his book, *Proof of Heaven: A Neurosurgeon's Near-Death Experience and Journey into the Afterlife*:

"Love is, without a doubt, the basis of everything … This is the single most important truth in the universe, but also the single most important scientific truth as well."

I do not profess to be an expert on Love. At the start of this year, I considered myself a love 'apprentice', with plenty of scope to learn more about love and draw it into my life, which inspired my journey. I'm sure I'm not the only person to embark on such a quest, but as Elizabeth Gilbert points out in her book, *Big Magic: Creative Living Beyond Fear*, "It might have been done before, but it hasn't been done by you!"

So, this is *my* take and experience on Love. Here's how it all started …

Inspired by the words of Leo Tolstoy, *"Each person's task in life is to become an increasingly better person"*, each year, I choose a word to theme my year. This word becomes the inspiration for my life that year, as I focus my attention on what this word means to me and how it can enhance my life through learning, and ultimately growth. This year, I chose the word Love. My Love Project simply started with a journal entry prompt each day:

"Today I showed Love by ..."

Some days were easy – I was the attentive mother and wife and 'kicked goals' at work. On the good days, I ticked everything off my To-Do List and felt great about myself. And other days went to crap. The interesting thing was, the easy days were just that – easy. But getting through the tough days while still feeling like I had shown love in some way – no matter how small – was where I found the accomplishment and growth. Despite exhaustion, frustration, and the overwhelming feeling of "I can't be bothered", when I coaxed myself to show *one small act of love* to myself or someone else, like reading a book to my kids, taking a long hot bath, or going for a run, I felt better. Even the smallest act was worth it.

Throughout this book, I will share how I have found, nurtured, and added more love to all aspects of my life. To make this book more actionable, I have included Love Lessons throughout. These are prompts designed to inspire you to incorporate more love into your own life. You will, of course, have areas in your life that are humming along nicely, whilst others need a little more TLC. This book is comprised of separate chapters that don't need to be read in sequential order – you can dip in and out of this book in whatever way suits your needs. I encourage you to focus on the chapters that resonate with you whilst adding your own focus areas. Let's begin ...

• CHAPTER 2 •

The Art of Self-Love

"Learning to love your whole self is the prerequisite for discovering your true nature and your reason for being alive at this time. Love is a language that all beings have in common. It is the language of the universe."
– JULIA PLEVIN, THE HEALING MAGIC OF FOREST BATHING

Find Your Flow

The older I get, the more I realise how much I need creativity in my life. Carving out time for creative pursuits I enjoy, such as writing, sewing, jewellery-making, and playing the piano is not only fun but essential for my well-being. This might be as simple as a couple of hours spent sewing on a Saturday morning or browsing through Pinterest for some fun handmade project ideas. On top of supplies, the two main things I need to make this happen are *time* and *space*.

To combat the 'time' challenge, in her book *Crappy to Happy: Love What You Do*, Cassandra Dunn suggests that, "You might grab a couple of hours early in the morning before the rest of the household is awake, or you might let the housework wait while you instead focus on writing a blog or creating art or studying something meaningful to you. The key is to prioritise those activities that engage and energise you at every opportunity."

Although finding the time to be creative has been challenging while trying to juggle the needs of my young family, it does get easier as the kids get older. I enjoy doing creative activities with them, such as colouring in, craft, and cooking. I can often find a simplified version of what I'm doing for them to enjoy and develop their skills, such as colouring simple pictures or sewing with forgiving materials such as felt.

The challenge of space has been resolved by converting our fourth bedroom into an office and sewing room. The space in our house is too precious to dedicate an entire room to a permanent guest room, especially when we don't have frequent visitors. However, we still have the capacity to accommodate guests as and when they visit.

Finding activities that put us into a state of flow are essential for our well-being. These activities don't have to always be creative, although they most certainly can be. Flow activities are tasks you become so engrossed in that it's like being in a time warp – hours fly by without you even noticing. These activities are mentally engaging and stimulating but not stressful. For example, after one particularly challenging day at work, I came home, sat down, and started writing, which instantly made me feel better. When I sit down to write, the world could end, and I wouldn't notice. I get so engrossed in what I'm doing I lose track of time and forget to stop for breaks. This is '**Flow**'.

Love Lessons:

1. How to find *your* Flow

A helpful way to identify your 'flow activities' is to recall the things you enjoyed doing as a child. If you can reintroduce these activities into your adult life, it is highly likely you will rediscover your state of Flow. Flow expert Mihaly Csikszentmihalyi, and author of *Flow: The Psychology of Optimal Experience,* advises, "It's a wise parent who allows her children to give up the things of childhood in their own time".

The Magic of Goal Setting

"Take up one idea. Make that one idea your life.
Think of it, dream of it, live on that idea.
Let the brain, muscles, nerves, and every part of
your body be full of that idea and just leave every
other idea alone. This is the way to success."

– SWAMI VIVEKANANDA

I have been setting annual goals for a number of years now and believe they are vital for personal growth. Goal setting is an act of self-love, as it helps you to determine what's important to you in life.

To plan my goals, I use an Excel spreadsheet with a separate tab for personal and business goals for each year, for example, *Personal Goals 2021* and *Business Goals 2021*. All tabs are kept in one document titled 'Goals', so I can easily flick between tabs and refer to my goals from previous years. Reflecting on what I have achieved over the last few years is an incredibly empowering exercise.

My spreadsheet also includes a column to record the steps I'm going to take to achieve each goal. This is key, especially if the goal is a big, hairy, audacious one. I sometimes split one massive goal into a few smaller, specific ones.

For example, 'Get Fit' might be broken down into:
1. run 5km x 3 times per week;
2. weight train at the gym once a week; and
3. swim 1km every week.

Breaking big goals down into smaller, manageable steps makes them less overwhelming and much more achievable.

In his book, *High Performance Habits: How Extraordinary People Become That Way*, Brendon Burchard shares the story about writing his book. He was curious to learn the best way to write, publish and promote his book, so he interviewed several number-one bestselling authors to determine their recipe for success.

Brendon recalls, "I simply asked, 'What five major moves made the most difference in moving your writing forward and landing your book on the big best-seller lists?'" Once he identified the common moves, he says, "all my effort went into those five moves. I stopped almost all other activities. I set up a calendar for accomplishing each activity. The first one, finish book, consumed almost 90% of my schedule for some time. After I got that done, most of my week was blocked so I could do deep work on the other activities. I sequentially completed those five moves. Everything else was classified as either a distraction or something to delegate."

We should work through our goals in the same way as any other project, such as writing a book or building a business. Brendon's advice is key: "You can do the same thing. Find the successful people you want to emulate in some way, and discover their five moves ... it doesn't matter whether you know how to achieve your Five Moves at first. The important thing is that for every major goal you have, you figure out the Five Moves. If you don't know the moves, you lose."

While I would recommend setting both long-term goals (5-10 years) and short-term goals (3 months-1 year) in advance, goal setting of any kind – from a business plan to your daily To-Do list – is beneficial. If you're new to goal setting, starting small is completely fine.

A really helpful tip I picked up from Matthew Michalewicz in his book *Life in Half a Second* is to write down three things you have done to work towards your goals each day. I keep a daily journal, and for those who want to keep it brief, this could be a complete journal entry. The reason I find this so helpful is that it isn't about completing the goal – it's about the small steps you take towards your goals. The three steps could be for one goal or three different goals – it doesn't matter. The key is to keep moving in the right direction.

On the days I can't record three steps or any steps towards my goals, I try not to beat myself up. Instead, I reflect on what happened that day and why it wasn't possible to complete the three steps. Perhaps it was because I was distracted, or my family needed me more than other days because of illness, etc. I can then recognise a pattern for my behaviour. For example, maybe I went to bed late or had one too many glasses of wine the night before, so I felt sluggish the next morning and slept in. This had a knock-on effect because I missed my early morning work session and played catch up all day. The lesson? Go to bed earlier and consume less wine on weeknights!

While the occasional 'blip' is ok, when we start to notice unhealthy patterns or habits creeping in, we need to recognise the impact these have on our goals and address them accordingly. If days go by without any work towards a specific goal, I then question the relevance of the goal and why I am avoiding working on it.

Know when to hold or fold

"Persistence is a valuable strength, but sometimes it can cause you to doggedly pursue a course of action when you might be better off dropping a goal or changing direction."

– CASSANDRA DUNN, CRAPPY TO HAPPY: LOVE WHAT YOU DO

Over the last year, I committed myself to some things that didn't serve me well. What appeared as 'exciting opportunities' at the time gradually grew dull as they sapped my time, energy and sanity.

I thought I knew better than to chase after 'bright shiny objects', but sometimes it is hard to distinguish ephemeral sparkle from great opportunities. The trick is knowing when to let go, something I have always struggled with. From a young age, my parents emphasised the importance of commitment. If I chose to do an extracurricular activity as a kid, I needed to stick with it. Quitting was not a word our family used, and if we couldn't commit to something properly, then we didn't sign up. Flippancy was not tolerated, and stickability was an essential character trait.

My commitment has been strengthened by inspiring stories of struggle and persistence, such as Thomas Edison's creation of the light bulb. In *Success Habits*, Napoleon Hill writes, "Mr Edison failed over 10,000 times before he finally discovered the secret of the incandescent light bulb. Can you imagine anybody going at anything and failing 10,000 times over a period of years and still sticking by it? Could you do it? Do you have any idea, my friends, how many times the average person has to fail in anything before he makes up his mind that maybe in the first place he didn't want to do that thing, but something else? As a matter of fact, it doesn't average one time because 50% of the people or more quit before they start. They anticipate that they are going to fail, and they don't even make a beginning." 10,000 times?! This takes commitment to a *whole* new level.

Another example, offered by Mel Robbins in her book, *The 5 Second Rule: Transform Your Life, Work, and Confidence with Everyday Courage*, is the story of Picasso's commitment to his craft: "Picasso created nearly 100 masterpieces in his lifetime. But what most people don't know is that he created a total of more than 50,000 works of art … that's two pieces of art a day. Success is a numbers game. You are not going to win if you keep telling yourself to wait. The more often that you choose courage, the more likely you'll succeed."

The above examples are the reason why I have always struggled with 'calling it' when something isn't working. This is problematic, as working hard at something for the sake of remaining committed can be unhealthy when an activity is draining your energy and ultimately impacting your health. The key is learning how to differentiate between 'weathering a rough patch' vs. 'flogging a dead horse'.

On his podcast, *The Brendon Show*, Brendon Burchard discusses when and what to quit. In his episode, *Quit the Wrong Thing Now,* he identifies three reasons to quit something, which are:

1. "Identify what makes you bored or miserable, and that which makes you come ALIVE". If you've given something a red-hot crack and it still doesn't float your boat, it's time to move on.

2. "Think legacy". Picture yourself at the end of your life and reflect on what you've done and what you're proud of. If this 'thing' doesn't' cut it, then it's time to quit it.

3. "Release those who are not ready". This point relates to the people in your life. People grow and change over time, sometimes in different directions and quitting relationships that no longer serve you is okay too. The key, says Brendon, is to quit decisively. Own your decision and move onwards and upwards.

Often the challenge lies in choosing between two or more options and quitting the rest to preserve time, money, and sanity. In this instance, Brendon advises identifying two projects that feel equally important right now, eg writing a book or starting a blog, and asking the below questions, then rating your answers 1-5 (with five being the highest).

1. Being Goals – if you do this, it will develop character in your life, will make you a better person, aligns with your self-expression and what is unique to you and gives you self-satisfaction.

2. Connection Goals – is one better for your relationships and bringing you closer to people?

3. Creating or Giving Goals – giving or contributing is the same as creating. In order to give something, you need to creatively express yourself. You are creating something that contributes or gives to the world.

4. Growing Goals – which one of these things would genuinely stretch you? Which one is outside your current ability and will bring struggle? That is, will it force you to develop new competency, meaning, knowledge, skill, ability, confidence. Which one is really going to push you?

Brendon concludes by saying, "The one that scores higher is going to be the one that gives you that intrinsic sense of meaning. It feels right for you to do".

Fill your life with experiences, not things

I've always been a fan of spa treatments such as facials, pedicures, and massages. However, in the last few years since having kids, a spa treatment is one of my favourite gifts to receive from family and friends. I feel so rejuvenated after being pampered, and it also gives me some quiet time to myself. After dealing with the constant barrage of clutter that enters our home on a daily basis, it is also refreshing to receive a gift that I don't need to find a 'home' for.

I regularly request a facial voucher for occasions such as Mother's Day, my birthday, or Christmas to ensure I get this experience at least once a year. I understand treatments are not for everyone – a lot of people don't enjoy being touched by strangers. However, think about an experience or activity you love doing or would love to do more if you had the money, time, or support, and add this to your wish-list the next time someone needs a gift idea for you. If it is too expensive for one person, suggest they split the cost with other friends or family members. This makes gift-buying easier for others and gives you a gift you really want.

Love Lessons:

1. Happiness Booster

Think about the things that make you laugh. For me, this is comedy. A few of my favourite comedians include Kitty Flanagan, Michael McIntyre, Graham Norton, as well as shows such as *Have You Been Paying Attention?*, *Gogglebox,* and *Hughesy, We Have a Problem* to name a few. For some reason, no matter how stressed or distracted I am, laughter really helps. Apparently, it's impossible to feel grateful and depressed at the same time, and this is how I feel when something really funny makes me laugh. Find *your* Happiness Booster and add it to your tool kit for difficult days.

2. Take yourself on a date

There is a quirky little café on the south-side of town I adore but rarely go to as it is out of my way. On one rare occasion, when I was working in this area and finished early, I took myself there for a treat. I rarely have the opportunity to sit in a café on my own, but when I do, I absolutely love it. This particular café has a warm, wooden interior and small tables, which give it a cosy, intimate feel. I think it is important to feel comfortable spending time in our own company, especially in public. We shouldn't feel uncomfortable about going solo to see a movie or having a coffee by ourselves. We've become accustomed to being surrounded by people at work, on our commute, or at home with our family. When we're not with other people, we turn to our devices for entertainment. I believe many children in western cultures have lost the ability to entertain themselves or simply be on their own without an external form of entertainment.

Sometimes it's beneficial to have quiet time on our own without feeling like we need to engage with others – in person or on social media. Reading a book, going for a walk, or making time for creative pursuits (such as writing or drawing) are simple ways to relax in our own company.

3. Identify your happiness senses

Smell, sight, touch, hearing, and taste are the five senses that most of us use every day, but is there one sense you particularly enjoy using? For me, many of my emotions and memories are triggered by scent.

One of the most poignant experiences I have had with scent was meeting my husband, who, for no reason I could explain, *just smelt right*. I'm not alone when it comes to feeling attracted to someone because of their 'scent', one that isn't created by an overpowering aftershave, that is. In *The Scent of Desire*, author Rachel Herz writes of Estelle Campenni, a psychology professor from Marywood University who recalls, "I knew I was going to marry my husband the minute I first smelled him." There are numerous studies supporting the impact our pheromones (compounds secreted by animals, including humans) have on our behaviour and physiology. Herz explains, "Your MHC genes determine your unique immune system and also your unique odorprint, and your odorprint is as unique as your fingerprint". Therefore, it is understandable that certain people would be attracted to other people with a specific scent.

I love perfume and trying different scents. I relish the perfume section at airports or in department stores where I can wander and discover new scents. I also reacquaint myself with old favourites, which evoke fond memories of the time when I wore that particular perfume. I was waiting for a prescription at a chemist one day, so I took some time to peruse their perfume section and smell a variety of different perfumes. I picked up one that looked vaguely familiar – Charlie White.

Instantly, I was transported back to summer 2000, my first summer in England. Smelling this scent was like opening a treasure chest of memories stored at the back of my mind. I evocatively remembered many of the places I went and even the outfits I wore – in particular, a music trip to a beautiful country house with the school orchestra from my GAP year. These were precious memories I hadn't recalled for years. While I enjoyed *smelling* the perfume again, I didn't want to *wear* it again for fear of losing the precious memories associated with it – rediscovering it had been such a joyous experience.

• CHAPTER 3 •

Love the Skin You're In

*"Take care of your body.
It's the only place you have to live."*

– JIM ROHN

Taking care of our body is not only essential, but also one of the greatest ways we can show love to ourselves. In this chapter, I will share how I used movement, nutrition, sleep, self-care rituals, and more to nurture my body throughout my *Year of Love*.

Self-care is self-love

The perception of self-care being 'selfish' or 'vain' is gradually changing. My grandmother was of the opinion if you spent too much time in front of a mirror, you were 'vain' or 'idle' and had nothing better to do with your time. While my grandmother always looked smart, she was very practical when it came to her appearance and the time she dedicated to herself. I suspect this was typical for women of this generation, who were still reeling from the aftermath of World War II, the loss of loved ones, rationing, and making do without throughout this challenging period.

When this generation settled down and started their families in the late 1940s and early 1950s, the focus was on stability and homemaking, not tripping the light fantastic. But along the way, I feel women in particular neglected their own needs by putting those of their families first. It's not surprising this generation are often referred to as the 'silent generation'. Their martyrdom continued as their children, later known as the 'baby boomers', made their way into the world. They often supported them financially through university and tertiary education, providing them with opportunities they had never had. Although women from the boomer generation were often limited in their choice of career path, with many studying and entering the fields of nursing or teaching, they had more choice and education opportunities than their mothers did.

Once her children had flown the nest, my grandmother continued her homemaking duties, supporting my grandfather while he worked and in his retirement. My grandfather was a kind, capable man and contributed to many household chores, like washing up, but my grandmother was the household's driving force. While she seemed content in her homemaker role, I believe if my grandmother had studied or pursued a career, her self-care perspective would have been very different. In fact, I don't think the term 'self-care' was even in her vocabulary.

We have come a long way since my grandmother's generation and now understand by not taking the time to implement self-care, we are at risk of not functioning at our full capacity, or at worst, burning out.

Our knowledge of nutrition and the benefits of physical activity have been expanded over the last few decades. While previous generations anecdotally knew they felt better when they ate good food and moved, we now have the science to support this. I believe the most significant hurdle we face going forward is changing the mindset that self-care is not selfish – it's essential for us to survive and thrive.

Mastering Movement

I discovered exercise (especially running) was my sanctuary after I had children. I joined a women's gym when my daughter was only three months old – the youngest age the crèche would accept babies after being fully immunised. In hindsight, it seems insane that I felt like exercising when she was so young. I could have been at home sleeping, but there was something inside me that not only needed to get out of the house but also have that uninterrupted hour to myself.

Exercise is strange in the way it uses energy but also generates energy. I would always feel rejuvenated after a workout – it would give me the energy I needed to get through the rest of the day and sleep soundly, even if my sleep was disrupted at night-time. The feel-good endorphins exercise creates also helped suppress postnatal depression, which I could have easily slipped into after relocating from Melbourne to Canberra (where we knew no one), when our daughter was only two weeks old.

Running was also a powerful healing technique for me following the birth of both my children. Pre-children, I had run and enjoyed participating in fun runs, so returning to running postpartum gave me a goal to focus on. Running is a more challenging form of exercise during and after pregnancy and must be done with extreme care to avoid any long-term injury such as a prolapsed uterus. I was able to gently run more than halfway into my first pregnancy, ensuring I kept my heart rate low and didn't overheat.

However, I was only able to tolerate running for a couple of months into my second pregnancy. Running didn't feel right, and there were so many other low impact exercises I could supplement running with. Prior to my son's birth in April, I set my sights on running the Outback Half Marathon in July. Post-birth, I suffered from pelvic pain, so I revised my goal to the Sunshine Coast Half Marathon at the end of August that year.

After a few months off during and after pregnancy, learning to run again is a slow process and can't be rushed. For me, it was like learning to run all over again, which terrified me as I wasn't sure I would ever get there. The first run started as a walk, interspersed with gentle jogging for 30 seconds to one minute every five or so minutes. It was a good day if I could manage five minutes of running in total during a session.

I trained regularly prior to the Sunshine Coast Half Marathon, but in hindsight, I didn't complete enough long runs, so I struggled around the course on the day. New shoes that weren't properly broken in were swiftly tossed to my husband at the 10km mark and replaced with my 'old faithful's' and I dragged myself over the finish line. After the race, I spent half an hour on the floor of the shower with excruciating pelvic pain, convinced I had caused serious damage to my body. After managing to feed my son, I fell asleep for the rest of the afternoon. I have heard since it takes nine months to make a baby, then nine months for the body to recover, which I would wholeheartedly agree with after this experience. Fortunately, I recovered with no lasting injury.

    I have since returned to running and the gym, trying to do some form of exercise every day. Physical activity continues to play an essential role in my life, and I always feel better when I move. The benefits of exercise are widely known for combating lifestyle diseases such as obesity, heart disease, and diabetes. Still, I particularly like the connection between exercise and the brain, detailed in *The Nature Fix: Why Nature Makes Us Happier, Healthier, and More Creative*. Author

Florence Williams writes, "Among his dozens of influential studies are those showing that exercise causes new brain cells to grow, especially in areas related to memory, executive function and spatial perception. Before Kramer's work, no one really believed physical activity could lead to such clear and important effects. Now people everywhere are routinely told that exercise is the single best way to prevent aging-related cognitive decline."

Throughout my *Year of Love*, exercise was often one of the activities I would do to show self-love and take some time out for myself. However, I also learnt to show myself love by taking exercise easy on days I felt tired or unwell, such as walking instead of running - I was still moving and getting fresh air, so it was a win.

Rest days are just as important as training days, as they give your body the chance to repair and recover. Neglecting rest days can result in illness and injury, so often, the best way to show love is to show yourself compassion.

A YEAR OF LOVE

The Power of Touch

When you touch a body, you touch the whole person, the intellect, the spirit, and the emotions.

— JANE HARRINGTON

I am a very tactile person — I love being touched (and no, not in a creepy way). For as long as I can remember, I have always loved massages — from my mum's loving back tickles as a kid to facials as a teenager. Now I enjoy a professional massage to release tension, ease sciatic pain, and stop a migraine in its tracks.

One of the best discoveries I made as a new mum was the 'off-peak' massage special at my local shopping centre — $5 for ten minutes of bliss! I would time my children's naps with a visit to the mall, and once the sleepy small person was out-cold in the pram, would make a beeline for the massage shop. I hoped like hell my little one stayed asleep while I was pampered for ten minutes — even if that meant constantly rocking the pram while being rubbed.

Sadly, my local massage parlour no longer offers this fantastic deal, but other deals can be found, especially during off-peak times. You can also negotiate a shorter massage timeframe to save money, especially if you ask them to focus on one area, such as the neck or shoulders. Most massage parlours are happy to receive your custom, regardless of how long your massage is.

I aim to get a massage once a month, ideally two weeks after my chiropractic session, to reduce muscle tension and maintain a good level of movement in my neck and shoulders. I really resonate with Robin S. Sharma's philosophy on the benefits of massage: *'I take a massage each week. This isn't an indulgence, it's an investment in your full creative expression/productivity/passion and sustained good health."*

Healing Waters

"The way to health is to have an aromatic bath and scented massage every day."

– HIPPOCRATES

Another of my favourite self-care rituals is taking a long, hot bath – especially on cold winter evenings when I take a bath nearly every night. For me, baths offer so many benefits, such as:

Muscle relaxation – warm water for tired, sore muscles is what cheese is to wine – they are perfect companions. While a warm shower will sufficiently relax muscles, there is something more effective about immersing yourself up to your neck in a hot bath.

Healthy skin – warm water and steam from a bath helps to open the skin's pores, making it easier to remove dirt and absorb moisture. I like to add magnesium salts and essential oil (diluted in a carrier oil, such as sweet almond oil) to my bath. The benefits of essential oils used for aromatherapy are numerous, such as reducing stress and promoting sleep.

Reading time – I love to read in the bath. This is one of the few uninterrupted times of the day I have to myself once the kids have gone to bed. I haven't dropped a book in the bath yet, but I choose small, light-weight paperback books that are easy to replace, should the worst happen. For me, reading is a wonderful way to escape and relax, but you could also listen to music, or simply enjoy the sound of silence.

Improved sleep routine – getting into bed feeling warm and relaxed after a bath sets you up for a great night's sleep, especially if you are a light sleeper or prone to insomnia. A warm bath is a trigger for the start of my sleep routine, which I often follow with herbal tea and reading a few pages of a book in bed or journaling to wind down further.

Rehydration – I often feel thirsty after a warm bath, which encourages me to rehydrate with a glass of water or a mug of tea.

A couple of words of warning: while I enjoy a hot bath, hot baths can increase your heart rate, make you feel light-headed, and scold or dry out your skin by stripping the natural oils. Hot baths are also not recommended during pregnancy, so always double-check the temperature before jumping in.

A YEAR OF LOVE

Look Good Feel Good

*"If you look good you feel good,
and if you feel good you look great."*

– WONDERBRA

Spending time on your appearance can sometimes be misconstrued as vain and shallow. Many people believe we should be investing our time and efforts in our character rather than superficial things. I have always taken pride in my appearance and don't believe it has compromised my other values. I believe you can still be a decent person and look smart.

In *A Return to Love: Reflections on the Principles of A Course in Miracles*, Marianne Williamson writes that make-up and clothes can have a positive role in our lives if we use them with a loving intention. "The point is not to seduce another person but to add light to the world in the form of beauty and pleasure. The meaning of things is how much we use them to contribute happiness to the world. Clothes and other personal effects are no different than any other artforms. If we perceive them lovingly, they can lift the vibrations and increase the energy in the world around us."

The key to looking your best is discovering your own personal style. Choosing a personal style doesn't have to be a complicated process, more a process of elimination to determine which clothes, accessories, and make-up work best for your lifestyle. Here are some questions you can ask yourself to narrow down your choices:

1. What do you spend most of your day doing? For example, if you are working, where do you work, how do you get to work, does your work have a uniform or dress code? If you wear suits for work, identify a style or combination that works for you, such as a jacket and trousers or a jacket and skirt.

2. What colours do you like to wear? These could be colours that complement your complexion, colours other people have commented look good on you, or colours that make you feel good whenever you see them. Going one step further with the suit mentioned above, you could

purchase a suit (or shirts to go under your suit) in this colour or accessories in this colour to wear with your suit.

3. What is your body shape? Are there certain types of clothing you feel more comfortable in, or that fit and look better, such as trousers versus a dress or loose blouses versus tight tops.

4. If you wear make-up, which features of your face would you like to emphasise? Beautiful eyes with the right mascara or an incredible smile that radiates with the right shade of lipstick. If you don't currently wear make-up but would like to start wearing a little, start with something simple, such as mascara or lipstick. Both of these can be applied in under a minute and have a big impact, even if you don't apply anything else.

I am a huge fan of creating a 'style uniform' that works for your body shape and lifestyle. Your style uniform could be for work clothes, casual clothes, or both. Having a uniform reduces decision making and removes doubt about how you look every time you get dressed – especially if you are not confident about putting clothes together.

I created a style uniform when I was pregnant with my first child because I knew my body shape would change. I wasn't sure my body would return to the shape it was before pregnancy, and I wanted to remove any pressure on myself that it should, just because I had nothing in my wardrobe that fit. I wanted to be prepared for this change so I could embrace it and avoid grieving for my old life.

My pregnancy and immediate postnatal wardrobe consisted of lots of dresses in stretchy fabrics. I wore knee-length dresses that had some shaping around the neckline and bust. I opted for pleats that would expand over my pregnant belly, then gently drape over my postpartum potbelly. I sought dresses made from the finest fabric blends, such as viscose, bamboo and Modal, which felt luxuriously soft – I wasn't compromising on quality, as I wanted dresses that would last and look great long after pregnancy.

I found one particular dress style that worked well and bought it in several colours, including black. I then accessorised these dresses with scarves, cardigans and shoes that complemented the colours I had chosen. These dresses were comfortable enough to wear around the house and then could easily be dressed up with accessories when I went out. These dresses were made from a lightweight viscose stretch fabric that was machine washable and didn't require ironing – WINNING! Eight years on, I still wear these dresses regularly and feel as great as I did when I first bought them. You can use this same formula to find your own style uniform for any of your clothing requirements.

Love Your Locks

Before starting a family, I used to get my hair cut every three months. Now a mum, my time is more limited, and I'm lucky to get to a hair salon twice a year. I'm happy to colour my hair myself, but absolutely love the experience of getting my haircut by a professional. This was a self-care activity I rated highly throughout my *Year of Love*.

I book a haircut whenever I feel the ends of my hair getting dry or if it starts getting lanky – ideally 2-3 times per year. Knowing how amazing my hair looks and feels after a cut and blow-dry, I always try to coincide my appointment with an evening out with friends or other social events to maximise my enjoyment of my new, fluffy hair. Going home and chilling out on the couch feels like a cop-out after investing my time and hard-earned money on this luxurious experience, especially when I can't get it done as frequently as I'd like.

Love Lessons:

1. Look at your calendar to identify what social events you have coming up, and try to schedule your hair or beauty appointment earlier that day.
2. Make time to get your hair done at least once a year, and book it in advance, so it happens.
3. Enjoy every moment of your hair appointment. If you don't like talking to your stylist, take a great book or favourite magazine and politely let

them know this is the only time you have to catch up on reading.

4. If you have time and don't have children in tow, make a date with yourself and grab a coffee or lunch afterwards to maximise the experience.

5. Book your next appointment while you're there, and put it in the diary. You can always reschedule, but you'll be less likely to once it's in your calendar.

6. Try a few different salons until you find a stylist you love and trust. Then you won't have to explain what you want and hope for the best every time you get your hair cut.

Take Care of the Skin You're In

There are some things we all dread getting done regularly. The dentist is up there, but I make an appointment every six months and try to stick to it. Skin checks are another experience I find nerve-racking. I am fair-skinned, so I try to get my skin checked annually, and I have found the easiest way to do this is to pair it with something else I do annually, which is usually a trip to the Sunshine Coast to visit family.

Over the years, we have found a fantastic GP on the Coast who specialises in skin checks – my husband and I see him every time we visit. We feel like we have come to know him quite well, and he now has a detailed record of previous skin checks to quickly identify any alarming changes. Because most of his clients are from the Sunshine Coast, he is familiar with people who have seen a lot of sun, and he knows what to look for.

As we stay with family, we have people who can look after the kids for an hour or so while my husband and I go to get checked together and maybe have a sneaky coffee afterwards. I make the appointment as soon as we plan our holiday (at least a few months in advance) to ensure we get the date and time that suits us. By incorporating this mundane but necessary task into our holiday, we reframe it so it almost becomes 'fun' ... unless the Doctor finds something.

As with any other medical or physical check-up, this is one of the greatest ways you can show love and respect to your body.

Love Lessons:

1. Know what skin type you are and how frequently you should get a skin check.
2. Book skin check appointments in advance, so they don't fall off your radar.
3. Find a skin specialist you are comfortable with and try to see them for every skin check. They will keep records from your previous check and also become familiar with your skin type and lifestyle, such as how much time you spend outdoors.
4. Early detection saves lives. Get familiar with your skin and keep a track of any sudden changes to moles or your skin in general. MoleMap (www.molemap.net.au) have a handy ABCDE checklist:

Asymmetry – the shape of one half doesn't match the other.

Border – the edges are often ragged, notched, blurred, or irregular in outline; the pigment may spread into the surrounding skin.

Colour – the colour is uneven. Shades of black, brown, and tan may be present. Areas of white, grey, red, pink, or blue may also be seen.

Diameter – the size changes and usually increases. Typically, melanomas are at least 6mm in diameter (the diameter of a pencil).

Evolving – look for new moles or changes to existing moles.

5. Keep a photographic record of anything suspicious. This will help you monitor changes accurately.

6. Check your whole body – use a mirror or get a partner/family member to check your back and scalp. Moles can appear anywhere on the body … even in places the sun don't shine!

Don't put off skin checks, no matter what type of skin you have. The skin specialist will assess your skin type and let you know how frequently they want to see you. The most important thing is making an appointment – a skin check could save your life.

Dance Like Nobody's Watching

Dancing is a new form of movement I didn't expect I would ever enjoy as much as I have since having kids. I have always enjoyed dancing on a night out, but there is something more uplifting about dancing with your kids. If you are trying to encourage kids to move more, dance is definitively one fun way of doing this – the kids don't even notice they are 'exercising'. My go-to dance inspiration is Caleb Marshall's *The Fitness Marshall* dance workouts. I could grab a glass of wine and watch Caleb's choreography solely for the entertainment value. Caleb's energy is infectious – guaranteed to get anyone moving, even if it's just tapping your foot!

While holidaying with our family in Queensland this year, the kids and I giggled as we watched my 20-something-year-old sister-in-law and teenage niece perfect their TikTok dance moves. When they started googling dance videos for inspiration, I suggested they check out *The Fitness Marshall*. To my surprise, they hadn't heard of these dance videos, which then created an evening of 'dance offs' in front of the TV. We cast dozens of *The Fitness Marshall* dance videos onto the big screen and did our best to keep up. The kids had a blast and a laugh at our expense as they watched a bunch of adults showing off with their best dance moves. From the kids' perspective, we were listening to upbeat music, jumping around and having fun together. Three minutes swiftly turned into nearly an hour of energetic dancing, providing the ultimate workout.

Many people become increasingly self-conscious about dancing in front of others as they get older, especially if they have kids who tease them about their 'daggy' dance moves. Dancing is one of the best full-body workouts you can do, but most importantly, it's *fun*. Because we can dance with others, there are social benefits from dancing too. With so many different types of dance, from contemporary hip-hop to traditional ballroom, and folk, chances are you'll find a style you love.

This dancing experience made me realise we can show love for ourselves and others by taking the risk of looking foolish. The joy of sharing a special moment, like dancing with others, far outweighs the embarrassment of not knowing all the moves. The point is *participation*. So, flick the lights off, turn the music up, and dance like no one is watching.

Love Lessons:

1. Recall the last time you really enjoyed dancing. Where were you? Who were you with? What type of dancing were you doing?

2. How can you incorporate more dance into your life? For example, take dance lessons, join a dance class, find some online dance workouts or tutorials and schedule time in your day to do them. Arrange a night out dancing with friends or dance around the house with your kids.

Fuel to Flourish

One of the most common ways I show love is by cooking healthy food for my family. Home-cooked, healthy food not only nourishes us but brings us close together when we eat as a family. Eating together may not happen every night, and some days takeaway or something-on-toast is all we can manage. I am not a Master Chef by any stretch of the imagination, and I use of every pot and pan in the house when I cook, which is a constant source of irritation for my poor husband.

Slow-cooked or one-pot meals are my go-to favourites. There is something immensely rewarding about throwing a bunch of ingredients in a pot and letting time transform it into a magic melt-in-your-mouth meal. The kids still don't share my love of casseroles, stews, and curries, but they'll happily eat the rice or pasta I cook with it.

Reading *The Keto Reset Diet: Reboot your metabolism in 21 days and burn fat forever* by Mark Sisson reenforced for me the importance of how we fuel our body. Sisson explains a ketogenic diet helps you "reprogram your genes back to the original human factory setting of being fat and keto-adapted". Ketosis "is a state of metabolic efficiency where you are able to burn stored energy in the form of body fat and ketones, and not be dependent upon regular high-carbohydrate meals to sustain your energy, mood, or cognitive focus," says Sisson.

As a long-term sufferer of erratic blood sugar levels, the prospect of being able to 'normalise your appetite hormones so that you are almost never hungry' had me from the first page. I was fed up with having a bowl of cereal for breakfast, then feeling so light-headed and hungry by 10 am, that I could chew someone's arm off.

Reflecting on the advice given by my childhood doctors to combat my hypoglycaemia by eating a barley sugar when I did sport at school to keep my energy levels up, followed by a huge plate of pasta for dinner, the penny finally dropped. No wonder I felt like crap all the time – I was fuelling my fire with straw when what I really needed was a big log

I first noticed a difference in the way I felt on weekends after bacon and eggs for breakfast. I would feel full for hours – so full that often I didn't feel like lunch. I could also only eat one egg at a time as they filled me up so much. I never recognised that these high-fat and protein foods could be the secret to stabilising my blood sugar levels. I was, after all, a child of the 90s, when all fat was the enemy. Every weight-loss product was labelled as 'low fat' but still contained ridiculous amounts of sugar, and eating too many eggs increased your cholesterol. So, I spent years eating low fat and high sugar foods, wondering why I kept getting those blood sugar crashes.

When I first started reading *The Keto Reset Diet*, I started with one small change: swapping my cereal and toast to eggs for breakfast. Wow, what a difference this made! My 10 am sugar crash disappeared, and I wasn't ravenous when lunchtime came around. I also found myself eating smaller portions. For a month I used the diet as a guideline, although I didn't follow it to the letter, and also had a break from alcohol. While I don't believe I ever went into ketosis, as I still ate a bit of fruit, my diet was essentially low-carb, without alcohol, and I lost 3kg, bringing me down to my ideal weight.

It wasn't just about the weight though. My love handles disappeared, and my waist reappeared. The cellulite on my thighs reduced, and my thighs and butt looked more toned. My trousers became loose, and everyone remarked that I had lost weight. My skin glowed, and I stopped getting pimples. Above all, I felt *great*! I had so much more energy and wasn't thinking about food all the time. I still enjoyed food, but my hunger for my next meal built gradually. I no longer experienced the regular 'crashes' that I had accepted as part of my life.

The Keto diet isn't for everyone and often not sustainable long-term, which is why this book focuses on a two-week reset. After two weeks you can decide where to go from there. I think most people would feel so good by the end of the second week that they would want to continue some of their new healthy habits.

If you've been used to a high-sugar diet like me, moving away from this is really challenging. Full disclosure – throughout the first week of this diet, I felt like absolute crap. I knew this was my body trying to readjust and move away from my sugar addiction. What I didn't expect was how wretched I would feel physically. I had constant headaches, sweating, the shakes and was incredibly irritable.

Sisson warns, "you may experience a brief period of 'low-carb flu', characterised by symptoms such as low energy, headaches and brain fog. This is your body literally detoxing from carb addiction and working hard to transition to a fat-adapted eating pattern. Your brain, used to a fresh supply of glucose every few hours for years, hasn't yet built the metabolic machinery to burn ketones". It gets better though, assures Sisson, "With each passing day of ancestral-aligned eating, your fat-burning genes will upregulate and you will have more energy, focus, and appetite stability than ever before".

At one point, I did think I had the flu and should stop this diet. I questioned 'anything that makes you feel this bad can't be good for you, right?' But I assured myself this was a temporary side-effect and persisted.

The Keto Reset Diet book provides scientific evidence about why this diet is effective. Identifying the benefits, in addition to weight loss, is essential for reinforcing *why* you're making these changes. It is not just about weight loss but also about minimising inflammation and free radicals in the body. The book also acknowledges that our sweet tooth has evolved as "an efficient system of converting carbs into fat and storing them – to help us fatten up in the preparation for the scarcity of calories in the winter, and then access and burn stored sources of energy (ie, fat and ketones) for as long as necessary."

The problem with our contemporary lifestyles is that there is no 'winter', so most of us continue to binge on carbs year-round. The result of a long-term high-carbohydrate, high-insulin-producing diet Sisson explains is: 'daily fluctuations in energy, appetite, and mood; lifelong insidious accumulation of excess body fat (because you are bad at burning fat and are really good at storing fat, due to chronically excessive insulin production); a state of chronic inflammation in the body; and widespread cellular damage from glycation. Chronic inflammation, glycation, and oxidative damage are the essence of epidemic disease and accelerated aging in modern life."

Weight loss for many people is a simple equation of calories in versus calories out. Up until now, my strategy had been to focus on calorie expenditure through exercise. However, there are only so many hours in a day, which I swiftly realised when I went back to work after maternity leave. On the days when time doesn't allow for the luxury of a long workout, diet is the best way to control calorie intake.

The benefits of a keto lifestyle are that "you enjoy complete dietary satisfaction, rarely feel hungry (even if you skip meals!), and never have to struggle, suffer, restrict calories, or force strenuous workouts in order to burn extra calories. Instead, you allow your genetic setting as a fat-burning beast to naturally calibrate you to a healthy body composition. You will be able to properly utilize tools like Intermittent Fasting, nutritional ketosis, and ketone supplements to drop excess body fat whenever you want, without a struggle or a second thought," says Sisson.

Sisson also advocates the emotional benefits of the keto diet, saying, "Owing to enhanced oxygenation and neuron firing, ketogenic eating has been shown to reduce anxiety symptoms by 30 percent."

Love Lessons:

1. What are the unhealthy habits holding back your health at the moment? These could include overeating, excessive snacking, or poor food choices. Consider why these habits occur; for example, you work long hours and get home late, so picking up a takeaway on the way home is a convenient solution. An alternative option to this habit could be meal prepping on the weekend and stashing a bunch of meals in the freezer to eat on nights you can't or don't feel like cooking. Three minutes

in the microwave results in a nutritious meal and is quicker than picking up or getting a takeaway delivered. Soup is one of my favourite go-to freezer meals – it's quick to make and freezes well.

2. Keep some low-carb snacks on hand if you're craving sugar, such as nuts. I find macadamia nuts particularly satisfying because of their rich, creamy flavour. Another great snack is 85% dark chocolate; the higher the % of cocoa solids, the better.

3. Get inspired. We often turn to takeaway when we're feeling uninspired by our go-to recipes. This is when you know it's time to expand your repertoire. It doesn't require you to invest in the latest cookbooks either. There is now a plethora of recipes online, thanks to websites such as www.taste.com.au, or celebrity chefs, such as Jamie Oliver (www.jamieoliver.com), Nigella Lawson (www.nigella.com) and others. Your local library is also an excellent source for recipe books on any type of cuisine or cooking style, from keto to slow-cooked meals.

Sweet Dreams

'You snooze, you lose' is the motto that has always made me feel guilty for sleeping in or even going to bed early. While I have always known sleep was important, if work needed to be done, sleep was the first thing I would sacrifice to meet a deadline. Over the last few years, especially after experiencing 'small child sleep deprivation' when becoming a mum, I have realised how important sleep is for me to function productively. It wasn't until I read Arianna Huffington's book, *The Sleep Revolution,* that I fully understood the science behind sleep and why it is essential. Reading this book helped me identify what a 'good night's sleep' looked like for me. For example, I've learnt if I get to bed before 10 pm, I can get up at 5 am to squeeze in a couple of hours of work before the kids wake up. For me, two hours in the morning are worth four hours late at night when I'm tired and distracted by the day's events.

By understanding my sleep patterns and prioritising my sleep, I am more focused and less snappy during the day. It would seem I'm not the only one who is a nicer person to be around when I've had more sleep either. In her book *The Happiness Project*, Gretchen Rubin references a study that suggests, "getting one extra hour of sleep each night would do more for a person's happiness than getting a $60,000 raise". Wow!

However, the biggest benefit I have experienced from prioritising sleep is increased immunity. For me, personally, there is a direct relation to sleep deprivation and illness. I now carefully consider staying up late to meet a deadline or socialise, as I know it is likely I will pay the price with my health.

Love Lessons:

1. What does a 'good night's sleep' look like to you? Are you an early bird or a night owl? You can change from being a 'morning' or 'night' person throughout life, particularly as life circumstances change. I was a night owl at university but became

an early bird in my late 20s to avoid distraction from TV and social media at night.

2. Sleep routine – what is your routine before you go to bed? A quiet, restful routine before bed is conducive to a good nights' sleep. Indulging in a warm bath, drinking warm herbal tea (in addition to chamomile, there are various blends of night-time and Sweet Dreams teas available), reading a book, dimming the lights, as well as limiting devices and TV before sleep.

3. Consistency is key – a regular bedtime and wake-up time, even on weekends, will get your body into a healthy rhythm. Be mindful of late nights, and don't sacrifice your sleep for anyone! Sisson says, "Strive to get to bed at the same time each evening. The critically important deep sleep cycles predominate early in your sleep cycle, so sleeping in after staying up late doesn't quite cut it – even if you bag a similar number of hours. In an ideal morning, you will awaken naturally, near sunrise, without the need for an alarm clock, and you will feel refreshed and energized."

Support for Success

Regardless of how good our intentions are for our health, if we don't have the support of our nearest and dearest, the journey can be infinitely more challenging. Our family and friends don't need to embark on the same health regime as us, but if they don't support us by offering time and space for exercise or challenge our healthy food choices, they can hinder our success.

I have enjoyed running for the best part of fifteen years and have participated in over a hundred organised running races and fun runs. My wonderfully supportive husband has attended most of these, usually shivering on the sidelines to cheer me on and pass me a drink bottle as I run past. The conditions of many of the races I have attended have ranged from arctic-cold to blisteringly hot, with a bit of torrential rain thrown in for good measure. While I have been immensely grateful for his support, I'd often wish he'd participate as well or that there was a way I could reciprocate his loyalty.

A YEAR OF LOVE

Over the last few years, my husband's weight has crept uncomfortably closer to the 100kg mark. Halfway through 2019 he became ill – really ill for him. He was in bed for five days with flu-like symptoms and wasn't well at all. This took a toll on his body, as he couldn't eat for several days. At the end of this period, he had lost 5kg. This is often the only motivation my husband needs to kick-start a weight-loss regime. Over the remaining months that year, he not only managed to keep this weight off but continued to lose more.

Then the group of workmates he does group training with a couple of times a week decided to enter a Spartan Race. Preparing for this race as a group was all the motivation my husband needed to train consistently leading up to the event. He was apprehensive about the rope climb and a couple of other obstacles, but he nailed them all.

On the day of the event, the kids and I proudly followed his team around the course with the other spectators. I was thrilled to finally be able to return the favour and act as *his* 'support crew', as we cheered them on and took heaps of photos.

Love Lessons:

1. Set clear goals on how you want to improve your health. Choose any combination of fitness, diet, sleep, and relaxation that fits your lifestyle. If you want to make a lot of changes, it is advisable to start by making small, incremental changes. For example, if one of your goals is to run 5km and you've never run before, start by committing to a 30-minute walk and throw in a one-minute jog every five minutes. You can gradually build up from there. Likewise, 'eating healthily' could start with reducing the amount of sugar you consume each day or eating three plant-based meals per week. While going 'cold turkey' can work for some people, many find the drastic changes of a strict new routine too overwhelming and unsustainable for the long term. If you find the first few changes easy, you can always add more based on your long-term goals.

2. When embarking on a new health regime, rally your nearest and dearest to provide you with as much support as possible. Brief them on your

goals and how they can help you achieve them. They could accompany you on a walk or jog once a week, nudge you out of bed in the morning for an early morning training session, be open to trying healthier meals at home or cutting back on alcohol with you. The less temptation and the more positive influences you can surround yourself with, the easier it will be.

3. As the friend or family member of someone about to embark on a new health regime, offer them as much love and support as you can. Understand that what they are about to undertake won't be easy. There will be times when they are tired and irritable and just need a hug or a few encouraging words. Look for ways you can support them along their journey. If you usually catch up over a meal and a few drinks, suggest going for a walk together instead. If you are purchasing food for the household, prioritise healthy options and leave the tempting chocolate and chips at the supermarket. A healthy lifestyle is one of the greatest gifts we can give ourselves. Helping someone you care

about improve their lifestyle is one of the greatest gifts of love you can give them.

CHAPTER 4

Love What You Do

"Do what you love and you'll never work a day in your life."

– UNKNOWN

> *"The Atonement means putting love first. In everything. In business as well as everything else. You're in business to spread love. Your screenplay should spread love. Your hair salon should spread love. Your agency should spread love. Your life should spread love. The key to a successful career is realising that it's not separate from the rest of your life, but it's rather an extension of your most basic self. And your most basic self is love."*
> MARIANNE WILLIAMSON, A RETURN TO LOVE: REFLECTIONS ON THE PRINCIPLES OF A COURSE IN MIRACLES

I was sixteen when selecting subjects for my HSC (Higher School Certificate) and had narrowed my list down to six subjects when I realised that I was never going to be one of those people who had a single calling in life. I had interests in too many areas, which made focusing on one career path challenging. As the day when I had to decide if I was going to university drew nearer, I considered what subject area I might focus on, and eliminated all but two options: archaeology and fashion design. An Arts degree it was then.

In the meantime, my best mate and I were selected for a GAP year program at a school in Devon, England. This break from education was just what I needed to consolidate my thoughts about my future while becoming independent.

Our year abroad was more action-packed than either of us could imagine, and within nine months of living there, I could see myself staying for more than a year. In fact, despite the dark and cold (we arrived in early January), to me, this country strangely felt like home. There were plenty of people with luminescent-white skin like me, a rarity in Australia – everyone I knew had glowing tans, and behind that curious accent was an exceptional sense of humour.

I started researching university degrees in both my areas of interest – archaeology and fashion design. There was an abundance of choice for both – London was one of the major fashion capitals, and the UK was home to a plethora of archaeological sites. In the end, I tried to picture my future for each career path; archaeology, hanging out in a basement wearing a white lab coat, dusting bones, or fashion, attending glamorous fashion shows with a fancy cocktail in hand. As a fashion-obsessed 18-year-old, the decision didn't take too long to make, and I began to apply for fashion degrees around the country. In the meantime, I organised some summer holiday work experience at a bridal boutique in the town closest to the school I was gapping at.

The owner of the boutique was a vibrant young woman and an excellent mentor. She also had another intern who was about to embark on a degree in patternmaking at the end of summer. Both offered excellent advice on which universities I should apply to, but most importantly, their encouragement and enthusiasm roused in me a burning desire to pursue this path. I was unstoppable.

I received offers from several different universities, and while London would have been the obvious choice, I knew the accommodation and cost of living would be expensive. I also wanted to continue my adventure by getting to know different parts of this wonderful country.

So, the University of Wales College Newport it was!

September is the start of the academic year in the UK, and with a heavy heart, I had to finish my gap year early and leave my bestie to go to uni. I travelled up on the train before accepting my offer to check out the campus, lecturers, and accommodation. The campus was located a few miles out of Newport in the historic village of Caerleon, which is home to some impressive Roman ruins, including an amphitheatre and baths. I was sold.

A few weeks later, I packed up, and my bestie and I were on the train from Devon to Wales for Orientation Week. My wonderful friend stayed with me for a couple of days while I enrolled and settled in. She also organised a sensational dinner with relatives who owned a Chinese restaurant in Cardiff – this meal, as well as doggy bags of leftovers kept me going for days.

My university degree was simultaneously one of the hardest but most rewarding things I have ever done. Anyone who ever thought a Fashion Design degree is a 'cop-out' or 'bludge' never met any of my lecturers. Because fashion sometimes has an 'airy-fairy' stigma, it felt like they worked us ten times harder than students on other courses just to prove a point.

The following three years of my degree were like a boot camp. In the first semester, I tried to make the most of my uni life by making friends and socialising, which involved numerous pub sessions. I finished the first semester with a grade C, and my parents, who were supporting me, told me in no uncertain terms that if there were any more Cs, I'd be on the first plane home. After that, I pulled my socks up and became a hermit for the rest of my time at uni.

I started commuting to London every month to visit my boyfriend (now husband), who I had met earlier that year – this was the only time I took off. I also secured several part-time jobs throughout my three-year degree to help pay for my cost of living and uni supplies. As I progressed in my course, the cost of fabrics and other materials increased in direct proportion to our lecturers' expectations.

A YEAR OF LOVE

Throughout my degree, I have focused on securing as many work experience placements as possible. I started spending all my holidays in London, and arranged as many 1 to 2-week work placements with fashion companies as I could. In such a competitive industry, I knew that experience and connections were essential. There were many talented students who graduated a year or two ahead of me at uni who simply couldn't find work. I knew moving to London when I finished my degree would be as vital as building my connections while I was studying.

In my second year of uni, I did a summer work placement with a top trend forecasting company, WGSN (Worth Global Style Network). Trend forecasting uses carefully curated data to forecast the direction of consumer and designer trends. It is used by designers and retailers to predict, for example, what colours people want to wear or use in their homes, as well as their lifestyle habits, and most importantly, consumption habits. WGSN offered an online subscription service for businesses and offered a free service for students and educational institutions.

I developed a great working relationship with my boss and the team at WGSN. When I finished my placement, I was offered more paid work with them over the next uni holidays and eventually a full-time position. This was one of the biggest career dilemmas I have ever faced: finish my degree, or accept my dream job. After many weeks of deliberating, I decided to complete my degree. I wasn't a quitter, and if I changed jobs in the future, I would need my full degree to secure employment. To this day, I always wonder 'what if', as it was such an incredible opportunity. However, I wouldn't trade the learnings and growth I have experienced on my current path.

My third year of uni was one of the toughest years of my life, with an immense workload and limited sleep to get through it. I frequently burst into tears for no apparent reason – probably from lack of sleep – and often found myself fantasising about sleeping for an entire day. But I was so determined to finish with First Class Honours (a High

Distinction) that I pushed on. I also knew it wouldn't be forever – the end was in sight. My course leaders were clear that High Distinctions were elusive and usually limited to one student per year, but only if the candidate was worthy. In my final year, three of us had our 'eye on the prize', so competition was stiff. My grit, determination, and lack of sleep paid off that year when I was awarded the coveted High Distinction.

It was a bitter/sweet victory, as the other students vying for this award were my two closest friends, and I felt we had all worked equally as hard as each other. One friend had young children, so in many ways I felt she had worked the hardest, trying to balance home and uni life simultaneously. I was, and still am, incredibly proud of this achievement. When times get tough, I reflect on the strength I mustered during this period. I know if I could make it through this, I can get through other challenges too. A High Distinction was also viewed favourably by future employers, so this was a wonderful way to start my career.

One of the work experience placements I had completed was in the buying office of the British Department store, Debenhams. Buying required a combination of business skills and creativity and was a career path that appeal to me. There was an abundance of retailers with buying offices based in London, so I felt confident there would be no shortage of work in the long-term. The week I returned to London, following several months at home in Australia preparing for our wedding and getting married, I received an email from one of the buyers I had done work experience with at Debenhams. A junior position had become available, and they encouraged me to apply. The opportunity came at the perfect time, and serendipitously, I was offered the role.

I worked at Debenhams for three and a half years. During this time, I was promoted and grateful for the opportunity to work across three different areas: lingerie, accessories, and swimwear. I had three very different bosses and learnt so much about the industry and working with other people.

I was mostly content in my role and adored the people I worked with, but couldn't help but feel something was missing. I had worked my backside off during my degree and often found myself questioning, "Is this it? Is this all there is?". The role was demanding and often stressful. A large part of my time was spent managing the production schedule. Invariably there would be delays caused by sourcing or factory issues, and tough conversations were often needed with suppliers. On top of that, we had a strict profit margin requirement we had to adhere to, so there was intense, robust negotiation on prices with suppliers. The constant 'back and forth', trying to shave a penny or two off a cost price, was exhausting.

My lowest points were the days I would pass the guy sweeping the street on my way to work and feel envious of him. He was just sweeping away, with seemingly not a care in the world (although I'm sure this wasn't the case). I would frequently get home from work and burst into tears. The people I worked with were lovely, and I had learnt so much, but my day-to-day role essentially involved relentless negotiation on cost prices and delayed production. It was gruelling, and I couldn't see how I was adding any value to the world by sending grumpy emails to overworked and underpaid production teams in China and India.

After eight years in the UK, my husband and I decided it was time to return home. We had been married for four years and were keen to buy a place of our own and settle back home in Australia before thinking about a family.

The same parent company owned Debenhams and a well-known department store here in Australia. My British boss was happy to make a phone call and put in a good word to help me secure a position when I returned home. A couple of weeks after returning home in November, I had an interview at their head office in Melbourne and was offered a position to start in January.

The offer came with a warning: "This position, while at a similar level to where you were in the UK, is a very different role with different expectations. Buying and product development is *very* different in Australia compared to the UK. Oh, and we've also had 150% staff turnover in the last 18 months … we're doing a lot of work on our internal culture at the moment." Ok … What was I getting myself into?

I started my new role on a scorching January day in 2008 while trying to look for accommodation close to the city. My husband was still looking for work, but he managed to find us an awesome one-bedroom apartment within walking distance to work and kit it out with furniture and other essentials. I started in the womenswear department, backfilling a position that had been suddenly vacated before Christmas. It felt like the deck was stacked against me from the beginning. No buying had been done for the brands I was in charge of for months, and any existing orders were running late. I had regular updates with the buying manager to try and get things back on track.

After a couple of months, my manager had recruited a permanent buyer for this area, and I moved over to sleepwear and intimate apparel, the area I was employed to work in. By Easter, my boss and assistant from that area had resigned, and once again, I was running a department I knew little about on my own. The department manager recognised I needed help and recruited a couple of other people, which did improve things.

I enjoyed working in this department – I loved the product and the camaraderie of my immediate team. Outside our little department, however, things weren't that great. The attrition of team members continued, and there were some other team members that made my life difficult. The work never ended. When my boss and assistant left, we were behind in buying, which meant many late nights spent at the office trying to catch up.

I was exhausted, and all the extra time spent at work was taking a toll on my relationship with my husband. I managed to talk my department manager into letting me have a laptop and a token so I could work from home. Suddenly I found myself answering emails at 11 pm. No matter how hard I worked, I couldn't shake the 200+ emails a day or get ahead with planning and production.

Once again, I found myself in the same position I had been in at Debenhams a couple of years prior and questioning the point of what I was doing. I could completely relate to Arianna Huffington's observation in her book, *The Sleep Revolution: Transforming Your Life, One Night at a Time:* "It's also our collective delusion that overwork and burnout are the price we must pay in order to succeed." I was completely deluded and burnt-out.

In her book, *Read Me First*, Lisa Stephenson acknowledges, "Battles drain us. If we are out there fighting all the time, we'll expend most of our energy on stuff that isn't or shouldn't be our priority. We'll be sitting in negativity. We'll be driven by the need to 'win' at all costs. We'll lose sight of what is actually important and what we really want." I felt like I was constantly in 'fight mode' – against suppliers and colleagues. Then I found a lump in my breast. After an ultrasound, it was determined it wasn't anything sinister, but this health scare was enough to make me realise this level of stress was not healthy *or* sustainable. It was at this point I knew it was time to make a change.

I started researching different career options, listening, and following the advice of icons like Jim

Rohn and Brian Tracy. I even read Richard Nelson Bolles' *What Colour is Your Parachute*. I decided the next best move was to develop my transferable skills, particularly in areas I was passionate about. My next career move wasn't obvious, but I knew if I continued to develop my skills, I would make progress.

Writing, I decided, was the main skill I wanted to focus on developing. I had always enjoyed writing and had received favourable marks in English at school and for written work throughout university. Writing was also a skill I could use in any job, although at the time, I had my sights set on fashion journalism. I found a reputable online course, which would give me the opportunity to pursue part-time work while studying.

As soon as I started the course, I knew I was on the right track – I absolutely loved the course content and assignments. I was encouraged by my course leader's positive feedback and the good marks I received. As for the part-time work, I knew I wanted to work in retail, but preferably for a smaller, family-run boutique-type business. I had worked in these types of businesses throughout university and preferred the personability and flexibility of small businesses. The expectations and responsibilities were usually higher in small businesses, but so was the opportunity to learn and grow.

I was offered a position as a part-time retail assistant for a wine boutique in the quaint South Melbourne shopping precinct. The store was within cycling and walking distance from our apartment, and my hours were 10 am-5 pm, which ensured plenty of time in the morning for study and exercise. My quality of life instantly improved. Gone were the long hours in the office or at home responding to emails at 11 pm. And the small team I worked with were absolutely delightful. For the first time in a long time, I felt valued and appreciated at work. For the first year I worked three days a week: Monday, Wednesday, and Friday.

I managed to complete my writing course and decided I needed some experience, so pitched to as many local and national publications as possible. This was 2009, two years after the release of the iPhone, and many people were embracing the technology smartphones offered. The social media boom had begun, and I could see an abundance of opportunity for online content for social media, blogs, videos and more. I secured a regular gig as a columnist for a local Arts magazine, writing a monthly round-up of exhibitions in and around Melbourne. Going to art exhibitions *and* writing about them – it didn't get much better than this!

Meanwhile, the manager of the store I was working for left, so I was offered the manager's position, which I happily accepted. My days increased to five per week, with the occasional weekend day, but I continued to work from 10 am-5 pm, which still allowed time for writing before work. I was the happiest I had ever been at work. I felt sufficiently challenged and appreciated – without the stress of long working hours.

I stayed in this position for three and a half years until I went on maternity leave with my first child. Over these few years, I had successfully balanced my full-time job with lots of freelance writing assignments and was proud of what I'd accomplished. I felt ready to take some time out to focus on my new role as a mum. I intended to take up to 12 months maternity leave and return to my job and freelance writing, but life had other plans for our little family.

Throughout 2012, my husband's work situation grew increasingly unstable. He was working in IT for a Government department at the time, and a number of redundancies had occurred throughout various departments. It was unclear how many redundancies would be made or which departments they would impact. To top it off, the IT job market in Melbourne was pretty slow at the time – not many companies were hiring, and there were a lot of candidates looking for work.

While my husband didn't get made redundant, the writing was on the wall. He felt it was only a matter of time, which prompted him to start looking further afield for suitable work. A recruiter approached him about a position with a government department in Canberra and flew him to Canberra for an interview. After the interview, I picked him up from Melbourne airport. On the car ride home, he received a phone call offering him the position in Canberra.

We loved living in Melbourne and had now purchased an apartment there, but we knew life was about to change dramatically with the birth of our first baby. The thought of escaping our cramped apartment in the big city to a house in a smaller city to raise our young family was appealing. With our daughter barely two weeks old, we packed up our apartment, farewelled the removalist truck and jumped in our car to drive from Melbourne to Canberra. To date, this has been one of our longest drives ever due to multiple stops for feeding, nappy changes, burping, pacifying, followed by more feeding.

With the prospect of returning to my retail position now off the table, it was time to focus on some of my other goals, such as starting my own business. An idea had been bubbling away in my head for a few months, and I'd undertaken extensive research to determine if it was worth pursuing. My maternity leave period was the opportunity I needed to reset and kick-start my online business. A word of warning for those about to embark on a similar journey – never overestimate the amount of 'spare time' you think you'll have with a new baby!

Eight years on, I am proud to say my business continues to go from strength to strength. It has transformed over the years, as growing businesses and people tend to do. Still, I am grateful for what I have accomplished, especially while juggling other commitments such as our young family and household, freelance writing, and other projects.

I have no doubt there are many other jobs I could do that would command a higher income but require me to work 9-5 (or more), five days a week. When I calculate the total number of hours I work in a week, it would come close to a full-time work week, including the time I spend working early in the morning and at night after the kids have gone to bed. However, starting my day early and finishing later (while still trying to get my full quota of sleep) means I can do the school drop off and pick up and make time for exercise during the day.

Right now, whatever I lack in 'income', I make up for in lifestyle and sanity. The older I get, the more I question my motivation for doing anything. Marianne Williamson's perspective on the reason 'why' we work really resonates as she writes, "When we are working solely for money, our motivation is getting rather than giving. The miraculous transformation here is a shift from a sales mentality to a service mentality."

At this present moment in my life, I believe I am in the best possible position to serve my family, customers, clients, and myself. This is the best way I know to show love through my work. On the tough days when I sometimes question my choices, I turn to a prayer featured in Williamson's book, *A Return to Love: Reflections on the Principles of A Course in Miracles:*

"Dear God, please give my life some sense of purpose. Use me as an instrument of your peace. Use my talents and abilities to spread love. I surrender my job to you. Help me to remember that my real job is to love the world back to health. Thank you very much. Amen."

Here's what I know about work so far:

1. Many of us work for 8+ hours a day – often more time than we spend with our family during the week. This is too many hours a day to spend feeling miserable, so find something you love doing or find a way to love it. I wholeheartedly agree with Elizabeth Gilbert's philosophy in her book, *Big Magic: Creative Living Beyond Fear:* "Do whatever brings you to life, then. Follow your own fascinations, obsessions, and compulsions. Trust them. Create whatever causes a revolution in your heart." Cassandra Dunn, author of *Crappy to Happy: Love What You Do,* also supports the importance of finding something you love doing, as she writes, "Pursuing work that brings you joy and meaning is not a selfish luxury. I want you to have the courage and confidence to pursue what matters to you and to know that you have a right to feel value and purpose. I want you to stop selling yourself short or telling yourself, 'it's just work'… I'm a firm believer that each of us has endless value to offer and that the world needs the gifts that you alone can bring."

2. University is not like work. At university, you are the customer – *you* are paying to be there. At work, you are *being paid* to be there. This alone makes a big difference between the university experience vs. the work reality. Universities can be tough in terms of workload and expectations, but they are generally very nurturing places. Their purpose is to inspire and guide you into full-time work. Everyone generally starts the course at the same time and therefore should be treated equally.

In the workplace, you usually start your career in an entry position and work your way up from there. However, the workplace is not an even playing field. Not everyone starts at the same level, with people coming and going from companies at various stages in their career, for various reasons such as promotions and pay rises, maternity leave, or working part-time to balance family life. The age difference in a workplace can also be more varied than a group of undergraduate students fresh from high school. A workplace will consist of people from different backgrounds and cultures who have studied in different fields to get where they are – it's a crucible of different personality types.

At university, the people I surrounded myself with were passionate and completely devoted to their course, as were my lecturers, who nurtured our enthusiasm. There were, of course, students who prioritised partying and didn't apply themselves, but I didn't have to work with them because we were graded individually. Don't underestimate the impact this will have on your experience in the workplace, especially when someone doesn't share the same work ethic or passion as you do or is simply having a bad day. Sometimes it's challenging to rise above the negativity in a workplace, no matter how much you love what you do. My workplace had 150% turnover in 18 months – that's a culture issue.

3. Dickheads are everywhere. Whenever I encounter difficult people, I chuckle as I recall a Jim Rohn quote that goes something along the lines of: "there are only a few mean people in the world … they just get around a lot". And they really do. I

have heard one of the most common reasons people leave a job is because of other people.

I have been on the receiving end of bullying in the workplace. The behaviour was subtle but persistent, leading me to question if it was really happening or if I was 'just imagining it'. I've since realised the treatment I received is known as 'gaslighting'. In the end I confronted one of the bullies. This was really hard, as many of the examples of behaviour I wanted to discuss with this person were small and seemingly petty, but when I started to record and write them all down, I could see a negative pattern. When I called out the behaviour, I was accused of being 'too sensitive' – a typical gaslighting response. So, I challenged this by saying that these behaviours were actually 'insensitive'. I reminded this person that workplaces consist of different personality types, and it would be best to consider this in the future. I also reported the incidents to HR. The bullying stopped, and I was proud I had stood up for myself and set clear boundaries with this person.

Whatever career path or job you choose, the days are long if you can't find joy in your work each day. You will experience tough days in every job, but every day you have the choice to either be miserable or make the most of where you are. When you make the most of where you are and 'whistle while you work', this is when you have the opportunity to touch others.

Cassandra Dunn acknowledges work ain't meant to be easy when she writes, "No matter how meaningful your job is, there will always be some tasks that do not feel like they are directly adding value. It's up to you to find the meaning and to focus on the valuable contribution you are making, even if that means you have to dig a little."

In *A Return to Love: Reflections on the Principles of A Course in Miracles*, Williamson tells a wonderful story of when she was working as a cocktail waitress and had the epiphany, "Oh, I get it! They think this is a bar! … This isn't a bar, and I'm not a waitress. That's just an illusion. Every business is a front for a church, and I'm here to purify the thought that forms, to minister to the children of God."

Mihaly Csikszentmihalyi makes a similar observation in his book, *Flow: The Psychology of Optimal Experience*, writing, "Of all the virtues we can learn no trait is more useful, more essential for survival, and more likely to improve the quality of life than the ability to transform adversity into an enjoyable challenge." Therefore, one of the challenges of work is being able to reframe the mundane, tough days and see the opportunity to add value to the lives of others.

Love Lessons:

1. When deciding on your career path, choose a direction akin to the things you loved doing as a child.

In *Big Magic: Creative Living Beyond Fear,* Elizabeth Gilbert asks, "What do you love doing so much that the words failure and success essentially become irrelevant?" Likewise, Rhonda Byrne suggests exploring your hobbies as a source of inspiration in her book, *Hero*, when she writes, "A hobby can be a clue to your calling, because it's something you're passionate about and that you make the time to pursue. Plenty of people's hobbies have turned into big dreams that became big companies."

Cassandra Dunn believes the clues lie in what makes us *curious*: "Rather than feeling pressure to pursue your passion, instead follow what makes you curious. What piques your interest? Most of us have some idea of the stuff we are interested in. When you walk into a bookstore, which section are you immediately drawn to? If there's a free seminar happening near where you live, what topic would you absolutely not miss? All these things are clues. Like a long trail of breadcrumbs, your only job is to stay open-minded and curious and keep putting one foot in front of the other without necessarily knowing where they may lead."

So, what lit *you* up as a child? You might have enjoyed painting or playing the piano throughout childhood; this doesn't mean you need to become a full-time artist or musician, but is there a way to incorporate art or music into your line of work? Alternatively, can you pursue this passion in your leisure time by making time to paint or play the piano regularly, take classes, or learn new pieces? Don't lose connection with the things you loved doing as a child. Devote time to activities that indulge your creative thinking. These extracurricular activities can help to reduce stress levels when other parts of your life or especially work, feel intense or out of control.

2. Seek work placements in your chosen field while you are at university to gain experience and confirm that the direction you have chosen is right for you. As discussed above, university life is very different from the real workplace. It is better to learn this before dedicating years of your life to an expensive degree. Also, consider what other paths you could take with your degree if you don't get your first choice of job when you graduate. It is advantageous to choose a degree with a variety of career options in case the market changes or *you* change.

3. Think twice before leaving a job because of one or two arseholes.

Chances are there are plenty of other people in your workplace who aren't arseholes and have your back. Unless you work in a small business and the person you don't get along with is your boss, look for other options. Can you change roles? Move to another department? Work different hours to the arseholes? If all else fails, confront them, or report them to HR. Often once you stand up to them and call out their behaviour (which can often be subtle), they will back off and find someone else to pick on. Unless you loathe the job and tasks involved, there is often a solution for dealing with arseholes. Cassandra Dunn presents some solid advice when she writes, "If you're unhappy at work, these are the choices available to you right now:

You can choose to leave.

You can choose to stay and actively focus on what's wrong, feel resentful and complain to anyone who will listen. (It's not an option I recommend, but I'm sure we can all think of plenty of times we've done this.)

You can stay and be proactive in changing the things you can and accepting the things you can't. Be grateful for the aspects of your work you genuinely appreciate and the people who make it easier. Remind yourself of your values and decide to live by them, even in the face of difficulty".

4. Whistle while you work.

"People who learn to control inner experience will be able to determine the quality of their lives, which is as close as any of us can come to being happy," explains Csikszentmihalyi. Think of five ways you can find joy in your work. This will be an easy exercise on the days you are crushing it, but this list is for the rough days. Some examples could include saying something kind by complimenting a colleague, customer, or client, smiling at everyone you encounter at work that day, taking pride in your workspace by cleaning and tidying around you. Listening to uplifting music and doing the very best job you can with every task you encounter – even the mundane ones. The key, as Williamson writes, is our mindset: "Our internal state determines our experience of our lives; our experiences do not determine our internal state." Cassandra Dunn also makes a similar observation, saying: "You can change what you do, you can change how you go about doing it, or, at an absolute minimum, you can change the way you think about it."

5. Upskill.

Find ways to enhance your work skills, either through training in areas specific to your work, or transferable skills, such as customer service, negotiating, or people management. Employers are often happy to subsidise courses and allocate time for training if you can demonstrate the additional value they add to your role. Instead of trying to improve your weaknesses, Dunn recommends focusing on upskilling your competencies: "Improving upon weaknesses is sometimes necessary and can be important for personal growth, but constantly doing things that don't come easily to you will undermine your self-confidence and erode your self-worth. You (and everyone else around you) will benefit from you identifying, developing and using your strengths," says Dunn.

Attending industry events such as trade shows, seminars and conferences is also another way to increase your knowledge and skills. This year I attended a *Grow with Google* event to learn more about using Google in my business. The event was informative, and I came away with lots of actionable ideas. It was also an excellent opportunity to network with the Google team and other local businesses. For me, however, one of the greatest benefits of this event was taking time away from my desk – being exposed to, and inspired by new ideas. Be selective about which events you attend, and don't use business events as a guise for procrastination or slacking off. Attending business events that support your business goals will help you see things from a different perspective and ultimately grow.

6. Share your knowledge.

The longer you work somewhere, the more knowledge you acquire about your role and the industry you work in. Don't keep this knowledge to yourself. Sharing knowledge through positive communication is the foundation of a healthy workplace culture. Look for opportunities to mentor new or junior team members to help build their confidence and company knowledge. Encourage peer-support programs where team members in similar roles can share their learnings and experiences.

7. You are not your work.

Because we spend so much of our day at our work, our work often becomes part of our identity. While work is *one* facet of our identity, it is not the *only* part. Life changes all the time, often unexpectedly. If what we do is so firmly entwined with our identity, and something suddenly changes, we can often find ourselves lost and facing an 'identity crisis'.

Dr Wayne W. Dyer puts it perfectly in his book, *Happiness is the Way*, when he writes: "You are not what you do. If you are what you do, then when you don't, you aren't. You don't exist. If you are your business, if you are how much money you make, if you are your home, if you are your family, if you are your children, then what are you when those things go away? They always do, of course, as life is very transitory. If your self-image is tied up with outside things, then when your job goes, when the house goes, when the children leave, when your spouse dies, whatever it might be, then you die a little bit too".

As Dyer explains, this applies to all areas of our lives – you are never 'just' a parent, or a home-owner, or an athlete, for example. Like a rare and precious gemstone, our personality consists of *multiple* facets.

Make a list of all the 'facets' in your life, such as the people and things you love, the activities you enjoy doing – all the things that add up to make you, you. A list of five to ten things, in no particular order, is a great start.

Keep this list somewhere safe and refer to it on the tough days; when you've had a challenging day at work, or the kids have been misbehaving. Look at all the other things on this list, and pick something else to focus your attention on. For example, if you have 'playing the piano' or 'running' on your list, make sure you do one of these other activities on a day when something else on your list has let you down. By doing this, we are reminded that our lives are rich with goodness, which we need to tap into on a regular basis.

"I don't think it's an unreasonable expectation to want to find joy and meaning in what you do every day. In fact, I believe it's your birthright. To define and express an ultimate sense of purpose through your life's work is a goal worth pursuing. It is intrinsically motivating. It is what Maslow referred to as the highest human need: 'self-actualisation'."

— CASSANDRA DUNN, CRAPPY TO HAPPY: LOVE WHAT YOU DO

• CHAPTER 5 •

Family: Where Life Begins and Love Never Ends

"The days are long, but the years are short."

– GRETCHEN RUBIN, THE HAPPINESS PROJECT

Family was the most important area of my life I felt that I could show more love for this year. In fact, on the first day of January – the first day of my *Year of Love* project – we had a family day out at a local water park, then went for a bike ride in the evening.

Family, especially young children, can test you when you're tired and have had a tough day, but the moments I spent with my family, no matter how small, was where I struck Love Gold. Some days, it was all I could do not to punch someone, and I'm not even a violent person! However, there were moments throughout this year I will remember forever because they were so spine-tinglingly special.

By taking the time to say to myself every day, "Today I showed love by ... ", and writing down an answer, I have captured those moments forever.

The stronger connections I fostered with my nearest and dearest throughout my *Year of Love* filled me with an overwhelming sense of gratitude for this experience. There were hundreds of incredible moments, but these are a few specific ways I showed love and developed deeper relationships with my family throughout the year.

One-on-One Time

When my children were babies, I remember another mother with older children wisely telling me that she found it essential to dedicate one-on-one time to each child. At the time, I didn't fully understand the concept. My kids loved each other and loved spending time together. My eldest loved 'mothering' her little brother, and her little brother was infatuated with his cool big sis. She always played with him and gave him her undivided attention. However, I quickly learnt that as my children grew and their personalities developed, they enjoyed playing quietly on their own, in addition to collaborative games.

My son and daughter play quite differently – my son loves cars and loud 'crashy' games, whereas my daughter often prefers playing role-play-style games, such as families or schools.

As children grow and develop, the benefits of having one-on-one time with a parent are more beneficial than I ever imagined. This 'sacred time' allows them to talk about things that excite or concern them or simply get something about their sibling or another family member off their chest – without interruptions.

One-on-one time doesn't have to be fancy. While morning tea at a café is fun, a trip to the supermarket is just as effective. All you really need is an allocated slot of time together and an open ear. No profound words of wisdom or advice are required – simply listening as they talk through a problem or fear is enough.

My children have formed their own friendships and are frequently invited to birthday parties without their sibling. This can be a source of envy and resentment for the child who isn't invited but also provides a unique opportunity for us to spend one-on-one time with the other child – either with one parent or both. Depending on the party, one parent can attend the party with the child who has been invited, while the other does something fun with the other child. Suppose the party is close to a shopping centre. In that case, one-on-one time with the child not going to the party could include morning tea, lunch or afternoon tea and a wander around the shops. If the party is near a park, quality time could be spent riding a bike/scooter, going for a walk, playing in the playground, or feeding ducks.

This year, the task of purchasing a gift for a party one of the children had been invited to also became a fun and convenient opportunity to spend one-on-one time together. After a trip to the shops to select the gift, we would then hang out and grab a treat, such as ice cream, frozen yoghurt, or sushi – a healthier option! However, there are plenty of moments throughout the day to spend time together; these were some other moments we enjoyed throughout the year:

1. Pampering – brushing your child's hair or trying out some new hairstyles, giving a manicure, pedicure, or foot massage.

2. Sharing a book together.

3. Legs up the wall, meditating or listening to relaxing music. If my daughter is feeling anxious before bed, I find playing relaxation music softly and lying with her while she falls asleep works wonders.

4. A trip to the park – on the couple of days a week I had at home with my son, we would try to have an 'adventure' on one of these days, which was usually a trip to the park. Some of the parks we went to had smooth, flat paths, so we would take his bike or scooter as well.

5. Shopping – The amount of 'toys' aka 'stuff' available to kids now is OVERWHELMING. There are infinitely more choices available than when I was a kid. As the kids grow older, I have become very conscious of every purchase we make. Despite my attempts to declutter, our home is overflowing with 'stuff'. The kids often have pocket money they have diligently saved, gift vouchers from birthdays or Christmas to spend, or we simply need a new pair of shoes or a specific item of clothing. A trip to the shops to source a key item is a great way of spending time together, but I wouldn't recommend a trip to the shops without a purpose. A shopping spree is fraught with danger – for your wallet and a junk-filled home.

6. Cooking healthy treats – like popcorn or mini muffins.

Learn Together

Like me, my daughter also has a creative streak which I try to encourage as much as possible. This year, she has been begging me to teach her how to sew. Sewing, especially on a sewing machine, requires a lot of time and my full attention, which I don't have an abundance of at the best of times. With the knowledge of what a big commitment this would be, I was reluctant to start. I also wanted her to learn to sew something easy, which she could use or play with, so her efforts were rewarded. What to sew though? I mulled it over for months with no spark of inspiration. Then scrunchies came back on trend – BINGO! Scrunchies are perfect for first-time sewers – they require minimal fabric and consist mainly of straight sewing. I don't know any girls who don't like scrunchies – even the grown-up ones.

Once we had decided what sort of scrunchies we wanted to sew, my daughter thought it would be fun to try and sell them to earn pocket money. This little sewing project was the start of an entrepreneurial journey as my daughter and I sat down to brainstorm her business idea. We thought about everything, from who our target market was to how much we'd sell them for, where we'd sell them, and how many we'd need to sell to cover the cost of a market stall and materials. We brainstormed a name for the brand, deciding on *Dolphin Designs*, which would specialise in scrunchies and hair accessories. We then designed a logo and business cards and created a Facebook page. I was astounded by how enthusiastic my daughter was – she asked all the right questions and had some incredible ideas. I don't ever recall being that switched-on as a seven-year-old.

We booked a market stall at a local market the following Sunday, invested in a pop-up gazebo, and set to work sewing as many scrunchies as we could in a week. Unfortunately, our first market stall wasn't the wild success we had hoped it would be. In hindsight, I'm not sure the people who shop at this market were our target demographic – think older, budget-conscious shoppers looking for a bargain.

Fast-forward a couple of weeks, and we signed up for a market stall at a local school fête. Our experience at this market couldn't have been more diverse. This market only ran from 10 am-2 pm, instead of 7 am-12 pm (with a set-up time from 5 am onwards) like the last market. But the most encouraging difference was that most of our customers were kids with pocket money they were itching to spend on something fun under $10 – my daughter cleaned up! I looked on with delight as she served girls her age and older, who were all swooning over her creations – the smile on her face was priceless.

The Wonders of Walking

I have many fond memories of summer evening walks after dinner with my mum and grandparents when I was a child. The walks were short, usually only a block or two, but this was a magical time of day. The earth was still warm, but the sun had lost its intense heat. We would admire people's gardens and wave or chat to neighbours as we walked past. The pace was deliberately slow and mindful. While this was a gentle, incremental exercise, the intent was to spend time together and unwind at the end of the day.

On our holiday to the Sunshine Coast this year, we visited a place close to my husband's heart – Point Cartwright. This stunning headland has a lighthouse and offers a trifecta of picturesque views: Mooloolaba on one side, the Mooloolah River mouth, as well as the popular Kawana surf-beach on the other side. There are grass patches perfect for picnics and a path that skirts around the edge of most of the headland. One warm, windless evening, we decided to go for an evening walk and watch the sun set from the headland. My husband's brother came with us, and both boys shared stories of when they were kids growing up in this area, surfing and riding their bikes around the headland. We spent some time on the beach at the point, and for a few brief seconds, were all completely in the moment. The kids enjoyed taking their uncle's 'secret shortcut' through the trees back to the car. But the true magic of this experience lay in the memories and stories my husband and his brother recalled and shared with the kids, who were equally as fascinated to hear them as they watched the sun sink over the water.

Mealtime Rituals

Confession time: we don't eat together as a family every night. Phew! – I've said it. Sometimes the kids are super hungry and need to be fed before us, or we will be eating something the kids aren't keen on, such as a spicy curry. In these instances, usually mid-week, I try not to beat myself up about the fact that our main priorities for the kids are bath, dinner, bed. After the kids are in bed, we will often crash on the couch in front of the TV with said curry and a glass of wine to unwind. This is a precious time for my husband and me to debrief the day.

When we do eat together as a family, it's very rewarding. Drawing inspiration from a leading authority in positive psychology, Martin Seligman, and his *What-Went-Well-Exercise*, we usually start dinner by asking, "What was the best thing about your day?" and answer in turn. The benefit of doing this type of exercise, Seligman explains in his book *Flourish* is, "We think too much about what goes wrong and not enough about what goes right in our lives. Of course, sometimes it makes sense to analyse bad events so we can learn from them and avoid them in the future. However, people tend to spend more time thinking about what is bad in life than is helpful. Worse, this focus on negative events sets us up for anxiety and depression."

Seligman acknowledges there is probably a sound evolutionary reason for this. Had we sat around in our caveman days, waxing lyrical about the joys of life, we may have become a tasty snack for a hungry predator or failed to survive the Ice Age. To combat this, Seligman suggests we should "get better at thinking about and savouring what went well". Seligman recommends, "Every night for the next week, set aside ten minutes before you go to sleep. Write down three things that went well today and why they went well. The three things need not be earthshaking in importance

('My husband picked up my favourite ice-cream for dessert on the way home from work today'), but they can be important ('My sister just gave birth to a healthy baby boy')." Next, Seligman recommends writing an answer to the question "Why did this happen?" next to each positive experience.

To simplify this for our young family, we focus on one positive experience each. If everyone is still paying attention after the first round, we take turns to say a couple more. The key to this exercise is that no matter how crappy your day has been, you can still find a glimmer of joy in your day. It might be a small act of kindness someone has extended to you throughout the day or something delicious you have eaten. There is no right or wrong answer. Focusing on the positive instead of the negative is an excellent expression of gratitude. It is also uplifting to hear about the positive things that have happened throughout the day for our nearest and dearest, even if our day has been less than satisfactory. There have been days when I have been so exhausted from work that eating dinner is an effort, let alone engaging with my family at the dinner table. On these days, in particular, this exercise has given me an enormous surge in energy and helped me reconnect with what's important in life.

Family Reunion

Just before Easter, my father's extended family organised a family reunion. I have never attended a family reunion before, but it was a fantastic experience, and now I am converted! Family reunions are a great way to:

Reconnect with family members you haven't seen for a while, and meet new family members, such as children and grandchildren.

Meet other sides of the family you haven't met before.

Share stories, family history, and memorabilia to induce warm and fuzzy feelings of nostalgia. A few of our family members had done extensive family tree research, so it was great for them to collaborate and share their learnings, as well as fill in any gaps they had. Some people also bought family photos and albums to share, which were the catalyst for many fantastic stories.

Celebrate older family members who usually have intriguing stories and pearls of wisdom to share. This also highlights the value senior family members provide as 'memory keepers' by sharing their experiences and precious stories. Hopefully, those who hear them will remember them and keep their memories alive once they are no longer here.

Celebrate milestone birthdays. The purpose of this gathering was to celebrate a significant birthday of a senior family member. Still, it became a special event for us all as we reconnected with immediate and extended family.

The above points reinforce why family reunions can increase everyone's sense of self-identity and belonging. Reunions might not be a wise idea for families experiencing conflict, as they may further inflame existing friction. However, in harmonious families, reunions can strengthen existing bonds. This event was such a positive experience. I was excited when our family recently received an invitation to a reunion for my mother-in-law's family later this year.

Unexpected Appearances

I will never forget the look of pure astonishment and joy on my daughter's face when her brother and I turned up to her athletics carnival unexpectedly. I remember the disappointment I felt one year when it seemed like I was the only kid whose parents didn't turn up to my athletics carnival. Despite my limited athletic ability as a child, I was prepared to give anything a go. I entered as many races as possible, as our school sporting house was awarded points for every race we participated in, even if we didn't win a place.

My daughter was only in year one, and this age group participates in all the activities as a class. We hadn't planned to attend, but we finished whatever we were doing earlier than expected, so we went along to cheer my daughter and her classmates on. We sat with them while they had lunch, then watched a couple more activities after lunch.

The kids were then told it was time to get on the buses to go back to school, but they could simply go home if their parents were there. Spectators and an early mark ... made my daughter's day.

School assemblies are another event I like to attend if I can. Each class at our children's school takes turns hosting an assembly, which means it's not essential to go to every assembly. When a class is hosting the assembly, the children in that year group usually take turns speaking, which gives them valuable public speaking experience. I was incredibly impressed with how clearly and confidently my daughter and her classmates spoke at the recent assembly they hosted. The week before the assembly, the children are sent home with a 'cheat-sheet' of what they need to say and are encouraged to memorise it beforehand, although I'm sure they rehearse at school too. I feel like I'm being a supportive parent when I attend as many school activities as I can. However, if I'm unable to attend because of work, it doesn't mean I'm *not* a supportive parent, so I don't beat myself up. If the parents of my daughter's friends attend events I can't get to, and vice versa, we take pictures of the children to share with their parents so they don't miss out by not being there. We all just keep doing the best we can.

Cut the Commitments

As soon as children start school, and sometimes even earlier if they attend Playgroups and childcare, the 'obligations' start to drift down onto unsuspecting, enthusiastic parents' shoulders. Fundraising events, volunteering for the school fête, the canteen, classroom reading, chaperoning school trips, coaching, etc. You name it – you'll be asked to do it.

It's a slippery slope that becomes all too easy to slide down, thanks to the dreaded 'parental guilt' that mothers are particularly vulnerable to. Don't get me wrong – volunteering is an essential service in our community, without which many organisations and initiatives would not exist. However, the more activities children are involved in, the more parents are encouraged to get involved or help out.

In The Brendon Show podcast, Brendon Burchard recalls talking to a friend's wife at a social gathering. This lady was involved in a lot of community organisations and felt overwhelmed and stressed all the time. She explained to Burchard, "I don't have time to focus on myself", to which Burchard responded, "You don't have time to focus on yourself because you just haven't chosen to focus on yourself. You haven't given yourself permission. You don't have to be on any of these things." She was exhausted all the time, and her health was suffering as a result. "If you actually cared about your children, you'd stop all of those," said Burchard. The woman looked at Burchard in shock, and he continued, "Because your children don't want to see you wiped out all of the time. You're going to be more compassionate, more fun, more playful with your kids if you're not wiped out all the time. Get rid of those things, and focus on the kids."

Burchard fervently believes these things aren't essential. "What's essential in your child's life is you present, energised, positive, focused, imparting good life lessons – all the other stuff is the architecture of society making you feel obligated. You have to question those things."

The trick for parents is determining where we can add the most value, and this doesn't have to be volunteering or leading every committee. If you have the time and want to be involved, select the activity you believe you could contribute to the most – through your existing skills or simply passion and interest. For example, I love craft and sewing and feel passionate about helping kids learn these skills. I also recognise many parents don't have the time or skills to do these activities with their kids at home. I have happily volunteered to lead craft activities with my daughter's Girl Guide unit before. The kids are thrilled with being able to make something themselves. I love seeing them learning new skills like using a hot glue gun while developing existing skills, such as using scissors to cut out intricate shapes carefully. Win-win!

First, establish *if* you have any time to commit to additional activities. Then decide how much time and how frequently. Rather than a regular weekly or monthly commitment, it could be volunteering in the school canteen once a term, umpiring a soccer match every three months, or going on an annual Guide camp for a weekend. Contributing *something* is better than nothing, and not at the cost of our energy and sanity. Our volunteering efforts for our kids should benefit them – not hinder them because we are exhausted from spreading ourselves too thin.

Finding Connection Through Everyday Activities

Anyone who has tried to engage their children in 'helping' with the vacuuming or other household tasks has often wished they hadn't when the task takes twice as long, or a small plastic Peppa Pig figurine is swallowed and lodged in an irretrievable place in the vacuum. Over the years, I have learnt there are some everyday activities kids can be involved in that don't require dismantling the vacuum cleaner.

On his birthday this year, my son received a cheque in the post from a grandparent that needed to be banked. The easiest course of action would have been for me to deposit this one lunchtime when he was at school. However, he had been asking about money and bank accounts, so I thought this was as good an opportunity as any for a lesson.

In the bank, we queued a little longer than my son would have liked (lesson #1 of bank interactions completed) to be served by the teller. When it was our turn, I lifted my son up so he could see the teller, and I explained what she was doing as she processed the cheque. Fortunately, she seemed to like children and enthusiastically explained how the process worked and even showed my son his account balance on the computer screen. Getting children involved in everyday activities helps them form a greater understanding of the world around them – especially if other enthusiastic adults engage with them.

Home, Sweet Home

There were a couple of days throughout the year when one of the kids was sick and couldn't go to school, so either my husband or I stayed at home with them. On one particular day, when my daughter had a temperature and sore throat but wasn't too sick, I set her up on the couch in front of the TV while I worked close by. I even insisted she have a nap after lunch to help her recover. Despite her illness and being a bit needy, I still managed to give her the attention she needed while accomplishing a satisfying amount of work — simply by being at home without interruptions. The errands and housework were put on hold, and I simply stayed at home and focused on what I needed to do. By the end of the day, I managed to lodge my personal and business Tax Return, as well as a bunch of other things; it felt GREAT! Reflecting on the productivity of this particular day, I vowed I needed more Home Days (ideally without the sick child) — at least once a month. However, this vow was swiftly forgotten, thanks to my varied work routine.

Making this monthly commitment proved to be tricky. Recalling the fantastic feeling of accomplishment I had at the end of that day has finally motivated me to block out a day in my diary. Over the course of a month, I am confident I can manage one home day – I just have to prioritise it. I think we could all benefit from home days, and here's why:

There are often fewer interruptions at home than there are in a workplace with colleagues, meetings, phone calls and emails.

A weekend day is probably the only Home Day option for people who work Monday-Friday unless they want to book time off work. Having a productive Home Day on the weekend will require advanced planning to minimise the distractions from your family. Work with your partner to successfully juggle kids and other activities and responsibilities.

Everyone's home environment and life situations are different, so a Home Day won't work for everyone. For example, if you are a single parent responsible for children when you aren't working, your version of a Home Day might be going somewhere quiet (such as the library or a café) regularly if you're doing work that requires your full concentration, or to a park or other outdoor space for focused exercise or relaxation time. The key is scheduling time to focus in a space where you can relax and won't be distracted.

Love Lessons:

1. Pick a project – personal or professional that has been hanging around on your To-Do List for a while. Break down the next steps to complete it, or at least get it moving and write down a Plan of Attack (POA). Next, look at your diary and identify a day you could focus on this and schedule it in – you will probably need to shuffle a few things around. The day before, review your POA so you are ready to hit the ground running on your scheduled day. Here's a helpful tip, prepare some quick and easy meals beforehand, so you don't have to

interrupt your flow by making meals throughout the day. Don't let anything like housework or even exercise get in the way. If you're anything like me, these activities are an excellent form of procrastination in disguise. Today you give yourself full permission to focus on this task until you have completed it.

2. Power Hour – If it is not realistic to dedicate a full day to your activity, an alternative could be one or two hours on the weekend. Gretchen Rubin often refers to a 'Power Hour' on her podcast, *Happier*. This is where you take a task (or tasks) that have been on your To-Do List for too long and tackle them in a one-hour sprint. It's an excellent way to knock off a bunch of small, annoying jobs or some steps towards a larger project. You'll be amazed at what you can achieve when you give yourself permission to focus. Another helpful tip for you; the less time you have, the more laser-focused you need to be. Let your family know in advance so nothing stands in your way.

Appreciation

Occasionally, my children give me small glimpses of their appreciation for all we do for them. One evening midweek, I encouraged my husband to go bouldering (indoor rock climbing), even though I'd had a long day and was incredibly tired. I think it is important for my husband and me to have our own interests outside the home and friendships with people we've met independently, not through each other or the kids. For me, those interests and friendships include my monthly book club and the occasional evening course. For my husband, it's watching rugby or bouldering with his group of mates. On the evening I had given my husband a leave-pass, my daughter could see I was exhausted and said to me, "Mum, I know it must be hard to look after two kids on your own." You have no idea! I thought.

Usually, two kids are manageable, but two kids who are equally tired and hungry after a long day at school, followed by after school activities, are an entirely different experience. However, I was impressed that my daughter had taken a moment to notice how I was feeling by acknowledging the situation and my mood. For the rest of the evening, she was helpful and compliant, which also had a positive influence on her younger brother. I felt my small act of love of letting my husband go out, despite how I was feeling, had been rewarded with my daughter's moment of emotional awareness.

Family Photos

Getting our family photo taken by a professional every year has been one of the most valuable investments I have ever made. The photographer we use every year was initially recommended by a friend, which, in my opinion, is the best way to find a photographer. Our photographer, Belle, has a fantastic rapport with people, especially kids and always gets the best out of us – especially when getting everyone to look at the camera at the same time; feels like 'herding cats'. We have had these photos taken every year since the kids were babies, and it has been a delight watching the kids change in the photos over the years.

We select around fifteen photos from the hundreds taken – no small task. Our photographer takes a mixture of family shots and individual ones of the kids or my husband and me. They are such a precious memento and something I'm sure the kids will treasure when they're older. Even now, at ages seven and five, they love sitting and looking through the photos from previous years and observing how much they have changed.

I believe paying for family photos every year is an investment in our family, ensuring our memories are captured and maintained. Most of us carry phones with cameras nearly everywhere we go. Some people have a knack for remembering to snap a pic when their child is doing something special. I am not one of those people. I cherish the 'magic of the moment' – not just with my kids but with anyone. As soon as I pull my camera out, the spell is broken, especially if I need to get others to pause and pose. For me, capturing a rare and tricky candid shot is the only way the moment remains intact.

The other challenge I have with family photos is getting everyone in the same shot. On the occasions we are all together, snapping a pic with everyone in it when there is no one else to take the photo is problematic if you're not a 'selfie master' like me. Unless you have a selfie stick, it is also challenging to capture anything but people's faces in a selfie, so details such as height and the clothes people are wearing are omitted.

Family photos are my way of ensuring we have at least one decent photo of the four of us, plus the dog this year, as well as some beautiful individual images of the kids. The photos are usually taken in early November to ensure there is enough time to get our family photo printed on Christmas cards to send to family and friends and additional photos of the kids for grandparents.

When I get photos printed out for the grandparents, usually using a photo machine at Officeworks or Kmart, I also get some extra copies for us. I have now started to put these photos in an old-style photo album for the kids to look at. The kids experience such delight from looking at photos of themselves and each other throughout their earlier childhood stages. Looking at photos also evokes fond memories and is an excellent prompt for recalling stories of the past for children, which they relish. Keeping photos in an album again has been such a hit in our household that I have started to go through the photos on my phone and print off the special ones. The idea is not to create a mountain of photo albums, especially when people are trying to minimalise and declutter. My aim is to curate a selection of photos that capture the most memorable moments in our year, alongside our professional family photos.

Love Lessons:

1. Consider the role family photos play in your life. Do you or your children enjoy looking at them and recalling fond memories? How can you appreciate these photos more?

2. Organise your digital photographs on your computer in an easier way to view, in folders by date or location.

3. Invest in photo albums. These can be procured for a reasonable price from stores such as Kmart, Target, Big W or Officeworks, etc. There are also options to create photobooks online from companies such as Vistaprint. Albums vs photobooks is a personal choice depending on the format you desire, as well as how much time and money you want to invest.

4. Make time to look at family photos with your kids: on a wet afternoon, when they need a break from screens, or whenever you update the album.

5. Update your albums at least once a year, or sooner if you are adding in pics from your phone; otherwise, the task will become too overwhelming and end up in the too-hard basket. I find a couple of months before Christmas, around the end of October, is a good time. You can also print out extra copies of pics for grandparents before life gets too busy over the Christmas period.

6. Think of other ways you can use photos to enhance your life. For example, display more photos in single or multi-photo frames around your house, or create a special frame with each child's photos for their bedroom. Don't limit your photo experience to your immediate family. Kids also love looking at photos of their grandparents and other family members when they were younger, which is a fun way to learn about family history. Be creative and enjoy looking back on these precious memories.

Halloween Treasure Hunt

One of the best things I organised this year was a Halloween treasure hunt for our kids and the kids next door. Halloween is a holiday we don't actively follow due to its American origin and the commercialised spin that accompanies it. I don't feel comfortable with the kids roaming the streets or terrorising neighbours for lollies. I understand many of the newer suburbs with young families are quite accommodating with decorations, signs, etc.

However, our neighbourhood is an established 1970s suburb with many of its original residents who don't celebrate Halloween.

Despite explaining my feelings to the kids, every Halloween they still resent not being allowed to partake in something 'all their friends are doing'. This year, I thought I would do something different, fun for them and manageable for me. I took a quick trip to the shops and purchased a modest number of lollies, some Halloween accessories that included long rubber witch's nails, witch's noses, etc., as well as a couple of loot buckets for collecting treasure. I created an imaginary witch character, then typed up some clues on the computer and placed these around the backyard for a treasure hunt. The kids from next door joined in, fuelling the excitement of hunting for the witch's treasure scattered around the garden.

It was a warm evening and time for dinner when we finished, so we ordered a Chinese takeaway and enjoyed this with our neighbours on the grass outside. All of this did require a bit of preparation, so I saved the document with the clues for next year. A memorable Halloween experience for everyone and something I would do again next year.

Love Lessons:

1. Think of a holiday or occasion you're not as enthusiastic about as others. What don't you enjoy about this occasion? For example, too much unhealthy food on occasions such as Easter or Halloween, the commercial aspect, or catching up with people whose company you don't enjoy. Consider how you can turn this occasion into a celebration everyone will enjoy: catch up in a different location, with different people, or swap the lollies for other treats, such as toys, pencils, colouring or activity books, etc.

2. Think of incorporating something else enjoyable with your activity, such as a treasure hunt or a delicious meal – home-cooked or takeaway.

Daytime Dates

One of my favourite activities is meeting my husband for a coffee or lunch during the day. My work often takes me into the city and close to the building he works in, so squeezing in a quick coffee doesn't take too much time out of our days and is an excellent opportunity to spend time together, no matter how brief. Having five minutes at home to talk, uninterrupted, to each other is a rarity at the moment, so a Daytime Date allows us to discuss anything we don't get a chance to at home. And if we have more time, we'll have lunch together – a lovely treat on a Friday.

Daytime Dates have made me realise it's not about the length of time we spend together that's important. The main thing is making time to have a break with each other – quality over quantity.

Love Lessons:

1. Consider how you can add more Daytime or Mini dates into your life with your partner.
2. Schedule these as recurring events, such as once a month on a Friday, and set a reminder the day before so you can ensure nothing prevents you from keeping your date.

A Need to Read: Reading with Kids

"If you want your children to be intelligent, read them fairy tales. If you want them to be more intelligent, read them more fairy tales."
— EINSTEIN

As a small child, listening to a story read by my parents was one of my favourite activities. I was fortunate to grow up in a house with lots of books, so it was never hard to find a captivating story. I was also allowed to listen to several audiobooks on cassette – Mr Men by Roger Hargreaves and Paddington by Michael Bond soon became firm favourites.

My world expanded when I learnt to read on my own. There is something delightfully independent about going to the library and selecting books you will read by yourself. I also relished reading before bed – this became a comforting activity I looked forward to every evening. My joy of reading was something I always vowed I'd share with my children, so they could experience the same kind of magic I had experienced as a child.

Fast-forward thirty years, and both my children have started their reading journeys. However, it is not as romantic as I recall ... my daughter has needed some extra help developing her reading skills. English is a bugger of a language to learn. Just when you think you've covered off all the rules, you'll encounter an exception. "Just sound it out" doesn't cut it for many words (now referred to as 'camera words', which can't be decoded and simply have to be memorised).

The curriculum of learning how to read has changed considerably since I was a kid. The teachers do a marvellous job, but mastering the English language can be a life-long pursuit. The most effective way I've found to engage my children in reading is by finding books that appeal to their personalities and capture their imaginations. Like other parents, I've quickly recognised some books and stories are timeless.

When they were small, my children would gravitate to books like *The Hungry Caterpillar* by Eric Carle or *Where's Spot* by Eric Hill. As they've grown, they have developed a fascination with classic tales by authors such as Enid Blyton, Roald Dahl, and J.K. Rowling. We've all enjoyed *Anne of Green Gables* by Lucy Maud Montgomery and C.S. Lewis's *Chronicles of Narnia*. Even though the language in original versions of books such as *The Secret Garden, Peter Pan* and *Little Women* is often hard to get your tongue around, my kids love the concepts and challenges introduced in these stories. All these tales present common life lessons: don't trust strangers (*Hansel and Gretel*), war (*Little Women*), sacrifice and working together (*The Chronicles of Narnia*), persistence and resilience (*The Secret Garden*), the joy of magic and imagination (*Peter Pan, The Wishing Chair, The Enchanted*

Wood, The Magic Faraway Tree, et al.) good vs evil (*Harry Potter* and Roald Dahl's *Matilda* series). In fact, if you think of any children's story, there is a message, a journey or transformation the characters undergo throughout the book. Books introduce us to the world, allowing us to observe it through different characters' eyes and their experiences. Many will remain in our hearts for life – our relationship with them so deep it is as if we are walking the same path they have walked before us.

In his book, *Solitude*, author Michael Harris observes how reading can help trigger compassion and empathy as he explains, "The parts of the brain that are involved with reading fiction in particular, share large areas with the parts of the brain that help us understand other people in daily life. When we read, our brains behave as though we are experiencing what the hero experiences. The solitary reader rehearses the lives of others, and I think that must be the definition of empathy – to rehearse the lives of others."

Reading abilities aside, immerse your children in these stories, whatever way you can, so they can benefit from the messages in these tales too.

Love Lessons

1. Make time for reading in *your* day. The best teacher is a good example, so if your children see you enjoy reading, hopefully, they will be inspired to read as well.
2. Make time for reading in *their* day. Reading doesn't have to be done before bed. It can be relaxing, but it can also be the last thing you (and they) feel like doing at the end of a long day. I found this particularly true when my eldest was learning to read. She couldn't deal with the frustration of deciphering words when she just wanted to go to sleep. Depending on your schedule, reading could be done in the morning before school, in the afternoon after school, especially after they've had afternoon tea and a moment to unwind. You could also read on the weekend when you have more time and patience.

3. Keep it fun. Reading should never be a chore, so bring joy to reading by finding topics you and your children are interested in.

4. Shorter is better. A little bit of reading regularly is better than a lot of reading less frequently. Kids have short attention spans, so reading one page and keeping them engaged is better than being distracted for a whole chapter.

5. Read as a family. Get older children to read to little ones. Little ones love the attention of their older siblings, and this is a great way for older children to practice their reading.

6. Explore different mediums. There are a plethora of audiobooks available today through Audible or free library resources such as Bolinda's Borrow Box. If I'm reading to each child separately, I will often set one up with an audiobook while I read to the other. Many audiobooks are read by the author or actors (my favourite children's stories are read by Kate Winslet), who are dynamic and engaging. There are also several websites with authors and actors reading to kids, such as Storyline Online and Play School Story Time. Watching

these stories is often an excellent way for kids to have some quiet time after lunch or at the end of a busy day.

Michael Harris provides an accurate summary of the benefits of reading when he writes, "At full power, a good book trains us to forgo our immediate environment. It trains us to sink into an imaginary space where its private life can thrive at the exclusion of all else. And importantly, as we separate ourselves from the world around us, we connect to something larger and far away, something foreign."

Take a Short Break

During every Christmas holiday break spent at home, we plan a day trip somewhere. Last year we went inland to Tumut, so this year we decided we'd go to the coast. On the third day into my *Year of Love,* we headed to our closest beach, two hours away. A four-hour round-trip in the car, plus three and a half hours on the beach, makes for a very long day, but it was perfect. We arrived at the beach mid-morning and spent hours playing in the waves, building sandcastles, and exploring rockpools until our sea-air-induced appetites drove us to find a late lunch. Sandy and sunburnt, with our bellies full of fresh fish and chips, we drove home – satisfyingly, the kids slept the whole way. We felt immensely grateful to be able to spend this day together at the beach – even more so twelve months later when this particular area was ravaged by bushfire. Our summer holiday day trip is something we will continue to do each year. It is a lovely family ritual and an activity we enjoy planning together. Although it is only one day, it is a special one because it breaks up our summer holidays and encourages us to step away from the jobs at home so we can spend time as a family unit.

Take a Longer Break

It had been many years since I had visited Norfolk Island, and a trip back was long overdue. Having spent most of my childhood years there, this picturesque island is close to my heart, and I always vowed I'd take my husband and children back there. The years had slipped by though, and we could never justify the cost of flights or get enough time off work.

Serendipitously, at the start of my *Year of Love,* when I looked at flights, I was astonished to discover they were on sale for a very attractive price. We then started to look at accommodation and found a large house in a secluded spot with breathtaking views across the ocean. The house was large enough to sleep six, but there were only four of us. Knowing how much my dad and step-mum love Norfolk Island, it seemed like an excellent opportunity to invite them along as well. We floated the idea with them, and a couple of hours later, they'd booked their flights too.

We scheduled our flights for late February. As fate would have it, the week before we were due to fly, a colossal cyclone developed in the Pacific. It hung around for quite a few days, and as a result, all flights to Norfolk Island were cancelled that week. If our flight *did* manage to take off, it would be the first for the week, and any spare seats filled with people from the cancelled flights, ie a fight to get on the flight. Despite checking in as early as we could to ensure we retained our seats on the flight, unfortunately, the airline did try to offload my dad. After some tense discussion, a few tears, and reiterating we were all travelling and staying together, we successfully negotiated to keep him on the flight.

It was a rocky landing on Norfolk Island, thanks to the turbulent weather from the cyclone, but we counted our blessings we hadn't been diverted when we discovered the pilot was only going to give it one shot. In addition to a few wet and windy days, the cyclone had a prolonged impact on the Island. The ship scheduled to deliver supplies to the Island was stuck offshore for days, unable to get close enough to unload her cargo safely. The supermarket shelves were near empty by the end of our stay. Luckily, we were still able to purchase lots of fresh produce. There didn't appear to be any shortage of delicious food in the restaurants, although I'm sure there was behind the scenes.

Aside from a few days of rain, which the Island desperately needed anyway, we still managed to spend plenty of time at the beach, sightseeing and chilling out. Unfortunately, our phones didn't work on the Island network, and internet access was expensive and limited. This made for an extremely relaxing family holiday that allowed us to unplug and reconnect.

A friend once told me she believed one of her biggest achievements in life was raising children that she actually wanted to spend time with and that wanted to spend time with her. I believe that getting to know your children is a life-long journey. We are all constantly growing and changing as we become older and have different life experiences. Many people believe they have an instant bond with their children when they are born. I wonder if this is perhaps a protective instinct rather than a bond with the child's personality, as personality takes time to develop and reveal itself. A person's characteristics are also partially formed as a response to their surroundings – nature vs nurture.

In her book, *The Happiness Project*, author Gretchen Rubin recalls a touching moment she shared with her daughter on holiday:

"On our last day at the beach, when we were packed up and ready to leave, Jamie and I sat reading the newspaper as we all waited for the ferry. Eleanor wandered off to practice her stair climbing on a short set of three stairs, so I went to help her climb up and down, up and down. I considered going to get a section of the paper to read as I stood with her – and then I realised, this is it. This was my precious, fleeting time with Eleanor as a little girl, so adorable and cheery and persistent, as she went up and down those wooden stairs. The sun was shining, and the flowers were blooming, and she looked so darling in her pink summer dress; why would I want to distract myself from the moment by reading the paper? She's already grown so much; we'd never have a tiny baby again." Rubin sums up childhood perfectly – it is fleeting and ephemeral. As tempting as it is to distract ourselves with the busyness of life, these moments are all we have, and day by day, they slip through our fingers.

The key things I learnt about 'showing love' to my family throughout the year were that small moments spent together doing everyday things, such as going for a walk, sharing a sunset or a meal, often have more weight than grander experiences, like going to an event or taking a holiday. I love Gretchen Rubin's take on happiness which could be compared to love in this instance, when she writes, "In many ways, the happiness of having children falls into the kind of happiness that could be called fog happiness. Fog is elusive. Fog surrounds you and transforms the atmosphere, but when you try to examine it, it vanishes. Fog happiness is the kind of happiness you get from activities that, closely examined, don't really seem to bring much happiness at all – yet somehow they do."

While the 'grand experiences' and time away from everyday routines and tasks certainly assist us in reconnecting, the purpose of my *Year of Love* was to instil love into as many everyday activities as possible and make it more regularly accessible.

When it comes to family, I firmly believe that love is an emotional investment – the more you give, frequently, the deeper and longer-lasting your bonds with each other will be.

• CHAPTER 6 •

Friends Are the Family We Choose

"Of all the things that wisdom provides for living one's entire life in happiness, the greatest by far is the possession of friendship."

– EPICURUS

One of our favourite things about our house and the area we live in is the strong connections we have developed with our neighbours and the local community. My first introduction to one of our neighbours was at the auction for our house, when he came up to introduce himself and said, "If you buy this house, you'll have great neighbours!". He wasn't wrong. We *were* successful at the auction, and four years later, we're grateful to call our neighbours our friends.

We have no shortage of neighbours. Our house is on a diamond-shaped block, so we share fences with six different properties. This could be a recipe for disaster, but we have been incredibly fortunate to find ourselves living alongside some fantastic people. Our neighbours are a mixed bunch of young families and retirees; most of the latter are original residents who have lived in the suburb since it was built in the 1970s. Such a dynamic mix has only added to the positive experience we have had living here.

Wine Time

We have especially connected with two of our neighbours, both retirees, over our shared love of wine. Both couples have travelled extensively and appreciate a good bottle of wine, so one of our social highlights is 'wine time' when each household takes turns in hosting drinks with nibbles. Everyone brings a nice bottle of something. It's been a wonderful way to get to know these two couples, as well as share some incredible wine. We have since converted the spare carport in front of our house into an alfresco entertaining area with a table large enough to seat 6-8 people. During the summer months, this is an easy place to host, as our neighbours will readily join us if they see my husband and me sitting out the front.

In early November, several local wineries near us organised a wine tasting event. I enjoy learning about new wines and understanding the production process. Tasting them is also pretty good too. Wineries and cellar doors are located in picturesque spots, so it's no hardship visiting them!

Knowing our neighbours love wine as much as we do, I suggested we make a day trip of it. We had the kids with us, and our 70+-year-old neighbours are not as mobile as they used to be, so we decided to take the day slowly and not rush. The first winery we went to was a grand country property that doesn't have a permanent cellar door. The tasting area was set up on the vast lawn at the front of the house, overlooking the surrounding countryside's stunning vistas. They had set up several tables with umbrellas, making it a comfortable place to sit and sip wine and take in the beautiful surroundings.

The next winery had an ornately designed cellar door with an eclectic interior, including a large, rustic wooden bar. The music duo, *The Awesome,* set the atmosphere with a selection of folk/jazz fusion tunes while we enjoyed a delicious platter on a table outside.

The next cellar door was set in a rustic shed and served freshly cooked pizza to order. The hosts were friendly and down-to-earth, and this winery had a real buzz as patrons sipped, chatted, and waited for their pizzas to cook.

Our final winery of the day had a stylish cellar door consisting of glass and modern surfaces framed by beautifully landscaped gardens overlooking the rolling hills in the distance. We returned home feeling satisfied with a boot full of wine. The day happily concluded with an early dinner of lasagne and a couple more drinks at our neighbour's house. It was a long day for the kids, but the advantage of socialising with our neighbours is that I could duck home early to put the kids to bed. At the same time, my husband stayed on to watch the rugby over a glass of whisky.

Our neighbourhood posy has continued to expand since a younger couple in their early 30s moved into the house at the end of the street. We often see them working in their front garden, and they have been friendly since they moved in, waving and smiling each time we walk or drive past. Because we host many of our wine and nibbles evenings in our 'alfresco carport', it has been very easy to extend the invitation and include our new neighbours for a drink and a chat. They've also said one of the things they love about living in this area is the connection they've made with all of us, so the feeling is mutual.

We also have a couple of young families as neighbours. It has been wonderful to watch our children form their own neighbourly friendships. One of the mothers told me she really values the friendships our children have formed. She believes friendships outside of school are essential, especially if one of the kids has experienced a tough day at school because they had a fight with a friend or were bullied by someone. At least they know they can always come home to another friend.

Schedule Social Time

I'll be honest, hosting anything at our house since we've had children has been one of my biggest challenges in life. It is impossible to keep an 'entertainment ready' house with two kids, even as they grow older. From baby toys to Lego and craft, I always need notice before people come over and die of embarrassment if anyone just drops in.

Over the years, I have identified a couple of benefits to hosting events such as BBQs, morning teas, dinner parties, kid's parties, etc., at home. Firstly, I love sharing our home with people. Secondly, nothing puts a rocket under my backside to clean up the house like having people over. This realisation has had a positive impact on my life because now I try to schedule a social event at home once a month – social interaction, *plus a* clean house once a month = win-win!

Other benefits of this scheduling include something for our family to look forward to, and developing relationships with people we care about. Inviting people into your home and personal space is much more intimate than meeting in neutral territory, such as a café or restaurant. There is also the value for money of eating at home, instead of buying a meal out.

We are very lucky to have a house with a pool. As much as my husband grumbles about the maintenance of a pool, this has been a fundamental drawcard for our summer entertaining, especially on blistering hot days. Our guests – adults and children alike love cooling off with a swim, and as a result, the pool has become the entertaining hub of our home over the summer.

Seek Social Opportunities

In Canberra, we are fortunate to have several lakes and parks that are ideal for walking or running around. This year during the warmer months (and Daylight Savings), I organised some evening walks with various friends. Not only was it an excellent way of catching up with friends I hadn't seen for a while, but it also fitted in some well-needed exercise that didn't involve a bottle of wine, unhealthy food, or an expensive night out. My only regret was that I didn't do this more frequently on the longer summer evenings. Our winter days are shorter, making evening catch-ups outside more challenging, but they are often sunny, albeit crisp. During winter, I try to schedule walking catch-ups on the weekend to make the most of the sunshine and daylight.

Love Lessons:

1. Think of creative ways to catch up with friends instead of the usual drinks and dinner, such

as going for a walk, run, or other types of exercise. For example, my husband meets a group of his mates for a session of bouldering (indoor climbing) every fortnight. Whilst they still go for burgers and beers afterwards, they feel better knowing they've done some physical activity first.

2. Look for new groups or activities you can take part in to extend your social circle, such as joining a book club, art class, exercise group, etc. Our Canberra Greyhound group organise regular pack walks for the dogs, which has been a really lovely way for me to socialise our dog and meet fellow greyhound owners.

3. Schedule regular time to socialise and catch up with friends. Humans are social creatures and require regular social interaction – the mental health benefits of connecting with others are infinite. I personally prefer catching up in person rather than over the phone or online. Still, anything is better than nothing, and the telephone or online video conferencing are a great way to connect with friends further afield.

4. Find micro ways to connect with people between catch-ups, such as sending a quick text or email to check in and let them know you are thinking about them.

5. Look for opportunities to meet new people through existing friends. Many of my new friendships have formed through old friends. Don't underestimate the power of 'friends of friends'. It makes perfect sense when you think about it – if you become friends with someone because of their personality type, chances are they have other friends who are like them – like attracts like. So, the next time you are at a BBQ at a friend's house, take the time to get to know some of their other friends – new friendships await!

"Let us be grateful to the people who make us happy; they are the charming gardeners who make our souls blossom."

– MARCEL PROUST

• CHAPTER 7 •

Friends with Fur, Wings, and Other Things

"Animals are wonderful, because they put you in a great emotional state. When you feel love for your pet, that great state of love will bring goodness into your life. And what a gift that is."

— RHONDA BYRNE, THE SECRET

The most exciting day of the last year was when I received an email from the local Greyhound adoption agency, advising me of a local greyhound trainer who may have a dog that would suit our family. My excitement piqued when I received an email from the trainer, saying she had a 28kg dog called Syd, who she thought might be a good match for us. He had been trained for a racing career, but he was a reluctant racer and didn't show much interest or racing potential. Perhaps he didn't have a strong prey drive like other successful racers. Whatever the reason, this was exactly the type of dog I wanted, and I was optimistic that our chickens would continue to have a peaceful existence. I arranged to drive to Goulburn the following Sunday to meet him – it was one of the longest weeks of my life. Ironically, that Sunday also happened to be Mother's Day.

The week before our meet and greet, I casually wandered up and down the pet sections in supermarkets and the Reject Shop, fantasising over what products I would need to purchase. I didn't want to go all-out, just in case he wasn't a match. If we did bring him home, I figured a collar and a leash would be essential for getting him in and out of the car, as well as a blanket for him to sit on in the car. I found a fleece blanket with a stylish grey leopard print on it that I immediately fell in love with and couldn't resist buying it – it was only $15 after all.

We woke early on Sunday morning, and I forwent my Mother's Day breakfast in bed. My son was eager to come with me, as was my daughter, but we only had room for one car seat and a dog in the back. My son has a long-standing fear of most dogs, particularly small jumpy ones, so I felt it was important for him to come and be part of the decision-making process too. I didn't want him to feel like he was being forced to share his home with a creature he was terrified of.

We set off just after 9 am, having arranged to meet at Goulburn Showground at 10.30 am. I was tense and nervous on the drive there – my head was full of questions, like: would we like this dog? Was I *really* doing the right thing? Would my husband warm to having a dog? Would he fit in the car? Would my son mind sharing the confines of the backseat with a large dog he had never met for over an hour? Yes, was the answer to the last question, but more on that soon. I put some upbeat music on and tried to relax.

The trainer was waiting for us when we arrived. She had a dog trailer, and after introductions, she went over to the trailer and opened a side door. A very nervous, awkward dog sheepishly jumped out of the trailer. She led him over to meet us, introducing him as "Syd". Syd seemed very shy and timid but enjoyed us patting him and rubbing his ears which the trainer said he loved. He had just been bathed, so he smelt fresh and clean.

The trainer asked if we would like to walk him, so we took him for a short stroll along the side of the racetrack. He seemed happy to walk with us and walked well on the lead. As we walked back toward his trainer, my son asked if he could hold the lead and walk him. I hesitantly said yes, and showed him how to hold the lead. All started off well until Syd suddenly pulled on the lead to sniff something on the ground, and my son freaked out.

He screamed and dropped the lead, which startled Syd, who jumped, and then realised the lead was dangling menacingly around his legs. This scared him even more, and he shot off across the racetrack! The faster we ran after him, the faster he ran away. We conceded that our chances of catching a sprinting greyhound were slim, so the trainer suggested we stand by our car as she calmly walked off to retrieve him. The poor dog eventually stopped and cowered behind a metal sign, thinking he was in trouble. The trainer said a few calming words to him, grabbed his lead and walked him back. Once she was back at her car and trailer, she motioned for us to come back over and we tried to make amends with more pats and ear scratches. My son wouldn't be on 'walking duty' for a while …

First impressions: although timid, Syd really was a lovely dog. He was very placid and calm-natured – exactly what I was seeking, given my son's fear of small, lively dogs. I asked him directly, "Do you think we should take Syd home?" and he quickly responded, "Yes, I love him". The next challenge was trying to get him in the back of our sedan. I was shaking with excitement, as well as nerves. I buckled my son into his car seat, then grabbed the stylish animal print blanket out of the boot and laid it down on one side of the back seat. The trainer led him around to the side of the car, but there was no way he was getting in. Having lived in a kennel with other racing dogs and used to being transported via a dog trailer, it occurred to me, he had probably never been in a car before and had no idea how to get in and out of one. Given he was so large, I was hoping he would sit still in the back. I vowed I would take it easy driving home and would stop as often as necessary to ensure a safe journey home.

The trainer helped me lift him in, but as soon as we started to put him in the car my son began to panic – crying and screaming. The trainer was very kind and explained that Syd wouldn't hurt him. Syd was just as nervous as he was, so we had to be calm for him. My son ceased his loud screaming but was still terrified as he whimpered from his seat … it was going to be a long trip home.

We set off slowly, but before we had even gone one block, my son started screaming again. Syd was still seated but had decided my son's lap would make a comfy pillow. My little boy was having none of it. We pulled over. I gently nudged Syd over to his side of the car, and we set off again. Within less than a kilometre, my son let out another scream from the back seat – this time Syd had stood up. We pulled over and I managed to coax him to sit back down.

We made it onto the highway without any further excitement. Both child and dog had seemed to settle a little. I put some music on and hoped everyone would stay calm for the one-and-a-half-hour ride home, but it was not to be. We reached a part of the road with some slight bends. Perhaps Syd was feeling car-sick or uncomfortable – either way, he found the need to stand up and reposition himself but lost his footing and fell down into the footwell. He was ok but was struggling to get back up onto the seat. This incident resulted in more screaming from my son. Syd finally managed to get back onto the seat, but by this point, my son was screaming hysterically. Out of fright, Syd managed to jump up onto the back parcel shelf. This was a sight to behold – a 28kg lanky greyhound wedged on the parcel shelf of our Ford sedan! My reaction to this bewildering sight was a mixture of horror and sheer astonishment. I also kept picturing my husband's smug face as he said, "I told you this was a bad idea", when we arrived home.

The only thing to do at this point was pull over. So, on the side of a 110 km per hour highway we stopped. I climbed into the back and coaxed the shaking dog down from the parcel shelf. Sitting between Syd and my son, I simultaneously cuddled everyone and offered reassurance in a calm, soothing voice. I explained to my little boy that we still had some distance to go, and if mummy was to drive the car without another incident like this, I needed everyone to stay seated and calm. It seemed to work. The rest of the journey home was uneventful, despite my severe shaking as I clung to the steering wheel, anticipating the next catastrophe.

As soon as we arrived home, we led Syd into the backyard to go to the toilet and familiarise himself with our yard. He was very nervous at first and whined a lot, which we've since realised greyhounds often do when they hear other dogs or want something. We brought him into the house, where he promptly urinated on my slippers – a source of great amusement for everyone except me. He sniffed around and scent-marked a few other places, not as inconvenient as my slippers though, thanks to our wooden floor. Feeding him was no problem since he had an insatiable appetite. However, we quickly learnt that not all supermarket dog food agreed with him … the odour from the backend of a 28kg greyhound can clear a room swiftly!

One of our biggest challenges was getting Syd to walk confidently on a leash. The leash was not the problem since he was comfortable putting it on and even walking with it. The challenge was his reservation when walking. He'd usually start ok, but then get one block from home and do the 'greyhound freeze', which is where he'd stop and refuse to walk any further – in any direction. This was extremely frustrating, given that he was too big for me to pick up and carry any distance. I'd try encouraging and coaxing him, I'd try being firm and pulling his lead, but sometimes nothing worked, and we'd just have to wait it out until he was good and ready to walk.

This went on for about a week when we first adopted him, so walks were initially very short. I had read it is advantageous to keep the world of new or adopted dogs, particularly greyhounds that are used to living in a kennel, as small as possible while they settle into their new environment. Limiting the number of new things gives the dog time to adjust to one new thing at a time. Everything from the TV to the vacuum cleaner, to walking around a neighbourhood with people, cars, and other noisy vehicles was all completely new to Syd. He coped remarkably well, considering.

Ten days later, everything changed. My daughter had Guides at 5.30 pm, and it was starting to get dark, but the kids were keen to take Syd for a walk. We decided we'd take him for a super quick walk around the block so we could maintain his daily walk routine.

As we left our house, we briefly chatted to our neighbour, who suggested we bring Syd next door to run around with their kelpie after our walk. We planned to do a quick lap around a nearby crescent. As we started to walk around the crescent, the kids spotted a medium-sized black muscular dog approaching us at pace. Not wanting to make any sudden movements, we stopped and waited for the dog to approach, hoping it would be friendly. When it was about a meter away, I turned side-on to the dog and said firmly, "No. Go home." The dog hesitated for a couple of moments and I repeated, "No. Go home." The dog turned as if to head back in the direction it had come from, then darted around behind Syd, sniffed him, and aggressively lunged, first biting his backside, then continuing to maul his side.

A little girl from the house the dog came from tried to call him back, but the dog ignored her and continued its frenzied attack. Syd didn't retaliate; he just tried to get behind me for protection. I tried to put my legs and body between the dogs but didn't want to bend over or put my hands between the dogs for fear of being bitten. I shouted at the dog and for help, then tried to kick the attacking dog several times, but that did not deter him. Knowing that Syd could run fast, I saw this as his best chance of escape. I let go of his leash and said, "run home Syd!" in the hope he could outrun this dog. Syd ran to another house on the corner of the crescent, but the other dog caught him and attacked him again.

Syd then ran up towards the main road with the other dog in close pursuit. Not wanting to lose them, I ran after them but lost sight of them when I got to the main road. At this point, I had left the kids behind and hoped they would follow me towards home. I continued to scream for help and could hear my kids behind me also screaming. I phoned the neighbour I had spoken to minutes ago, breathlessly pleading for help and asking him to meet us at the bottom of the street to help find the dogs. I found Syd bailed up against a car at the bottom of our street with the other dog still attacking him.

A teenage boy came running up the street with the little girl we had seen earlier. I said to him, "Is this your dog?! He's attacking my dog!" He grabbed the attacking dog by the collar and pulled him off. I asked him who the dog belonged to and he mumbled, "my uncle". Still holding the feisty dog firmly by the collar, he flipped it onto its back and swiftly disappeared with the little girl in-toe. They didn't stop to ask if we were ok, even though the kids and I were all crying and clearly very shaken.

Another man from a nearby house who had heard my screaming had jumped in his car and driven after us to help. He looked at Syd and said we needed to get him to the vet straight away. He said he knew where the attacking dog lived and said it had attacked other dogs before. The lady whose front yard the dogs had ended up in also came out and offered support. My kindly neighbour looked after the kids while I phoned my husband and asked him to come home urgently. I also phoned the local vet to explain what had happened and let them know we were on our way.

The vet was waiting for us when we arrived and rushed us straight into the consulting room. On examination, the vet noted several puncture wounds on Syd's right rear leg and around his anus. She also noted he had a high temperature and was very distressed. She cleaned his wounds and administered antibiotics and pain relief. A course of antibiotics was prescribed for the week to combat infection, which is very common with dog bites. Pain relief and anti-inflammatory medication were administered by injection. We were told to come straight back if his situation deteriorated. The vet also took photographs and a detailed record of his injuries.

Watching a gentle, defenceless animal being attacked in front of my six-year-old daughter and five-year-old son is one of the most traumatic things I have ever experienced. I was unsure how much I should intervene, not wanting to risk being attacked myself in front of my children, or worse, my children being attacked. I love dogs, but I cannot fathom why certain dogs behave aggressively towards one another. We didn't do anything to provoke this attack other than walk down the street that this dog lives in. This was an experience I hope never happens to Syd or us again.

The effect on the kids has been profound. The night of the attack, both kids woke crying in their sleep. Poor Syd spent the night on the mat next to our bed, clearly in shock, refusing to eat or drink, and whimpering in pain. At about 2 am I was still awake, so I jumped out of bed and lay next to him so my body was pressed against his. Almost instantly, he seemed to relax, as did I.

Sadly, these types of attacks are all too common in our communities. Since our experience, the ACT Government has imposed stricter rules regarding dogs off-lead, but attacks still occur when dogs escape from inappropriately fenced properties or people disregard the rules – it only takes one complacent dog owner.

Syd is still a very nervous dog, and it took many months before we could gradually socialise him with other dogs, especially dogs that aren't greyhounds. I was also a nervous wreck every time I saw a dog off-lead in the months following his attack. My heart still skips a beat when I see an unrestrained dog, but I try my best to remain calm as I'm sure Syd picks up on my anxiety.

> *"With the new day comes new strength and new thoughts."*
>
> – ELEANOR ROOSEVELT

As traumatic as this experience was, my personal growth has been immeasurable. I have a completely different perspective on dogs and dog ownership. I walk early in the morning to avoid other dogs (many people in our suburb walk their dogs after work). The hidden gift has not only been the well-being I've experienced by starting the day with fresh air and gentle exercise but also watching the sun come up. Watching the sunrise is one of the most magical experiences we can enjoy – and it's completely free. The dawn of every day offers new opportunities to start again, to try harder, or try something different. Every sunrise I am present for is revitalising and fills me with intense optimism about my life and the world around me.

I was also inspired to learn more about dog behaviour and was recommended a book, *The Other End of the Leash* by Patricia McConnell, PhD. This book reassured me that Syd could overcome his nerves around other dogs with gentle training and encouragement.

Adopting Syd has also (unexpectedly) increased my social network of like-minded dog enthusiasts. The ACT is home to a fantastic greyhound rehoming charity called Greyhound Connections. This not-for-profit organisation is run by volunteers and has an engaged Facebook community that supports dog owners and foster carers with advice and lots of cute greyhound pics. This community has offered tremendous support since we adopted our boy. Group events are also coordinated through the Facebook page, such as twice-monthly group 'pack walks'. These walks are an awesome opportunity to meet other greyhound owners and their dogs. I have made some wonderful friends through these walks, and they are a safe, healthy way to walk Syd while increasing his socialisation.

There have been many studies on the benefits of pet ownership, from companionship and increased physical activity from regular walks to mental health benefits. In his book, *The Little Book of Hygge: The Danish Way to Live Well,* author Meik Wiking believes that "Cuddling pets has the same effect as cuddling another person – we feel loved, warm and safe, which are three key words in the concept of hygge."

Kaara, a member of our local greyhound group, shares how her girl has helped her get through some mental health challenges: "Our girl has been such a blessing. I was diagnosed with depression and anxiety a year after she adopted us, and she never left my side during those first few very difficult weeks off work adjusting to the medication. She's also become even more cuddly than normal recently as she cosies up to her unborn human sister in my belly (currently 26 weeks pregnant)." When she's with her dog, Kaara says she feels,

"Calm, love, excitement! She's just so gosh darn cute!"

Eighty-five-year-old Mary continued to look after her husband's dog, Meg after he passed away. Mary and Meg had always been close, even though Meg was Jim's dog, but Mary and Meg became much closer after Jim's passing. Mary explains, "Meg helped me adjust after Jim died. She helped to fill the vacant spaces. She needed care and love too as she adapted to a new owner." Mary now also enjoys the physical and social benefits of walking Meg and says, "I have met many folk as I walk with Meg. I have what I call my dog friends, they are my neighbours who I didn't know previously, and I value their friendship. This is a bonus of owning Meg."

"If having a soul means being able to feel love and loyalty and gratitude, then animals are better off than a lot of humans."

– JAMES HERRIOT, BRITISH WRITER

Here's how to get more pet-induced goodness into *your* life:

Love Lessons:

If you don't have a pet, think of ways you can increase your interaction with animals, such as:

1. Walking a friend's dog when they are at work or going for a regular walk with a friend and their dog. Having a friend walk with Syd and me after his attack was incredibly reassuring. It helped relax me and rebuild my confidence, as well as his.
2. Pet sitting for a friend when they're away. Maybe for a weekend at their house or yours. It's a great way to get to know certain animals, especially if you are thinking about getting a pet.
3. Volunteering with an animal rescue organisation. There are plenty around, for cats, dogs, or both. Our local greyhound organisation runs a number of fundraising initiatives from Bunnings BBQs to Trivia Nights and sewing coats

for foster dogs; there is a job to suit any volunteer's skills. One of Canberra's local cat rescue organisations recently requested volunteers to assist with cleaning, feeding, and medicating the cats they have in care for a couple of hours one morning every week or fortnight. There are plenty of opportunities to volunteer, so reach out to an organisation you'd like to support.

4. Fostering an animal. If you are unsure about the long-term commitment of pet ownership, then foster first. There is an abundance of dogs and cats seeking foster care so that shelters can deal with other urgent cases, like animals requiring more intense round-the-clock medical care. If an animal is fit and healthy and just waiting for a home, they are often put into foster care until they find their forever home. It can take days to months unless you end up with the infamous 'foster fail' – an animal you fall in love with and welcome into your home permanently.

5. Getting a pet. This choice does require some serious thought, but there really is a pet for everyone. Our chickens are pretty low-maintenance and reward us with lots of delicious eggs and cuddles. We also don't have too much trouble finding someone to look after them when we go away because they are also rewarded with fresh eggs.

A pet also doesn't need to cost the thousands of dollars many breeders will charge. Purchase animals available through rescue organisations such as Pet Rescue and RSPCA. Kaara recalls why she and her partner decided to adopt a greyhound: "I wanted a puppy sausage dog originally and my partner thought spending $3,000+ on a dog was insane and suggested we adopt a greyhound. I hadn't even given this a thought before, but we went to meet a black and white four-year-old-girl who was up for adoption, and straight away, she picked us and we knew it was meant to be."

When asked if there were any pitfalls of pet ownership, Kaara said, "The only 'downside' to having a pet is that you can no longer make last-minute plans to go away somewhere... in saying that, those type of plans don't sound fun for us anyway, we love taking her everywhere with us. She's been on many a holiday down the coast, and she loves the drive to Melbourne too." Kaara believes the benefits of owning a pet far outweigh the challenges when she concludes, "Knowing we rescued such a beautiful little girl is the most satisfying feeling in the world."

> *"Until one has loved an animal, a part of one's soul remains unawakened."*
>
> – ANATOLE FRANCE, FRENCH POET

• CHAPTER 8 •

Home is Where the Heart Is

"This is the true nature of home – it is the place of Peace, the shelter, not only from injury but from all terror, doubt and division."

– JOHN RUSKIN

Our home is our sanctuary. Home is the place we retreat after a tough day, to connect with our families or seek peace and solitude. Throughout my *Year of Love*, I discovered many new ways to connect with my home and enhance my life and my family's. Rather than continuing to see our house as one big To-Do list of never-ending housework and clutter, I came to appreciate everything it and the things in it represented in our lives: shelter, comfort, a place to socialise and connect. Instead of focusing on the clutter and dust, I focused on the 'feelings' our house evoked at different times throughout the year: when we returned from holidays, during the summer when our house was kept cool from the shade of our lush, green garden, or in winter when the house became a cosy retreat from icy days.

I restored furniture, engaged a cleaner, found ways of making items in my home more accessible to recapture the joy of using them, and looked at my home with fresh eyes. When we express love and appreciation for our dwelling, it metamorphoses into a comforting cocoon to nurture us through our toughest days.

"Home is where one starts from."

– T.S. ELIOT

A YEAR OF LOVE

Repair and Restore

At the beginning of the year, I purchased a couple of second-hand pieces of furniture from a local church fête: a set of wooden director's chairs and a little wooden desk. I tackled the outdoor chairs first, as I knew exactly what I wanted to do with them: re-stain and recover. My husband had a leftover pot of stain in the shed from a previous project, so I rose early every morning for a week until I'd re-stained every chair. I had also found some gorgeous floral furnishing fabric on sale and used the previous covers as a pattern to make new covers. I'd picked up each chair for $5 (the same chair, new, was just under $50 in Bunnings), so I was delighted with the result.

My second furniture restoration project was a cute little wooden desk I wanted to refurbish for my daughter's bedroom. My daughter had been asking for a desk for her room for months, and she fell in love with it as soon as she saw it, despite its unloved state. It had a retro look with cute angled legs and a small draw. The size was perfect – it wasn't too high or deep, so wouldn't take up too much space in her already-cramped bedroom.

As with many of my 'projects', the desk sat in the garage for a few months before anything happened to it – mainly because I wasn't sure *how* I wanted to tackle it. In the end, I decided to repaint it gloss white – classic and pretty for a girl's room. I sanded the life out of it to remove as much of the previous peeling paint as possible, which admittedly took longer than I was anticipating.

Following the 10+ coats of paint and four cans of spray paint later, it was finally complete. I found a cute ceramic handle in an antique shop and covered the removable desktop with a pretty floral contact. When my daughter outgrows this desk, it will make a cute side-table, and I can simply change the contact to update the look.

The easier option would have been to pop out to Ikea and grab a flatpack kid's desk. Indeed, we had looked there a few weeks ago but couldn't find anything that would fit in my daughter's room. I was delighted she found this little desk and feel we have given it a new lease of life by lovingly restoring it. It also has more meaning to my daughter and our house because it wasn't a mass-produced, off-the-shelf purchase. Most importantly, my daughter feels special because I lovingly spent time on it for her.

A Room of One's Own

Our house often looks like a kids' playroom. While the open-plan style of our home encourages social engagement between our family and with guests when we entertain, we only have one main living space, which is challenging to keep tidy all the time. Our house has four bedrooms; the kids have a bedroom each, and we have the master bedroom. The fourth bedroom, rather than being exclusively a guest bedroom, has become a combination of my husband's office on one side and my sewing room on the other. Sometimes I feel selfish that we haven't turned this room into a playroom, but the kids *do* have their own rooms.

My husband and I happily share the master bedroom. However, I like our bedroom to be a place of rest. My husband works from home occasionally, so it is important he has the space to set himself up and is not disturbed by the rest of the family. While I have consolidated a lot of my sewing supplies, I would like the remainder to be accessible so I can sew regularly.

As there is no additional space for a desk, or my sewing gear, purchasing a folding sewing cabinet from a friend who was having a clear-out completely changed the way I sew. This clever cabinet, with a spot for everything from thread to scissors, pins, and more, allows me to quickly and easily access my sewing equipment anytime I choose. The sewing machine also fits on top of the cabinet, with its cover on to protect it from dust. Previously I had to store my machine in its box in the cupboard. When I wanted to use it, I had to move other items to get it out, set it up, and then move everything in the cupboard to put it away again. This was one of my biggest barriers to sewing, which was very frustrating, given it is one of my favourite creative pursuits.

Having all of my sewing supplies carefully stored in plastic crates, it wasn't until I acquired this sewing cabinet that I realised it's not about having *storage* for things that matters; it's how *accessible* things are. The accessibility of an item determines if we will use it or not.

Even though my sewing supplies were neatly organised in plastic boxes and I knew which cupboard my sewing machine was in, it was an effort to get everything out. The lack of accessibility sapped the joy out of using it all.

Similarly, one of the best purchases I made this year was a clear plastic A4 draw unit with five draws. This unit is *perfect* for organising the kids' pens, markers, pencils, crayons, paints, and other stationery. But most importantly, it keeps all of these supplies easily accessible and tidy.

Love Lessons:

1. What creative activities do you enjoy doing or wish you had more time to do?

TIP: If you're struggling with ideas, think of the creative things you enjoyed as a kid.

2. Consider why you don't do these activities anymore – what barriers are in your way, ie space, time, inaccessibility, etc.

3. How can you break down these barriers, ie schedule time for these activities, even if it's just thirty minutes or an hour on the weekend; create a designated space in your home to do your activity, or find a new way of storing the equipment and supplies for your activity so it's accessible.

Fresh Eyes

I am filled with mixed emotions when coming home from a holiday or mini-break. Part of me wants to avoid the reality of my looming To-Do list, but another part of me longs to be in my own space and bed so that I can get back into a routine. The last time we came back from a two-week holiday, we had been staying with family for most of the time, so I was longing for space and solitude. Over time, I have learnt I will either feel calm or stressed when we get home, and this is directly related to the state the house was left in before we left.

Trying to organise four people and their possessions for a two-week holiday is no walk in the park, so the house is frequently left in a state of chaos when we go on holidays – a 'future me' problem when we get home. This is not conducive to a tranquil end to our holiday, especially if we get home late in the day, and is further compounded when we dump all our luggage inside.

However, the last time we returned home, I was surprised by the feeling of peace I felt as I walked through the door. Had staying with family for two weeks affected me that much? The house smelt like home because it smelt like us. There were a few things lying around out of place, and our house is always cluttered thanks to two kids under ten, but our kitchen was clean and tidy, and oh how I'd missed our coffee machine! I loved reconnecting with the family photos and kid's artwork dotted around. I loved our hall stand, and despite being overloaded with hats, bags, and jackets, we use it every day.

An accurate way to determine the 'feeling' of your home is to note your first impression when you get home from a holiday or weekend away. Our home can become so familiar that it is hard to view it objectively like a visitor would when they visit your home for the first time.

Love Lessons:

This activity is not about what other people think of you or your home. It is about looking at your home from a different perspective and trying to improve the things that aren't quite right in your personal space.

1. Each time you go away for an extended period, get into the habit of doing the Fresh Eyes test when you get home. As you approach your house, what are your first impressions of your front entrance? Consider:

Is it warm and welcoming?

What is the current condition of your front door and entrance area – is it clean and free of spider webs and dust?

What colours are you greeted with? What colour is your front door and surrounds?

Could you soften your front entrance with accessories such as pot plants? A new doormat, door wreath, etc.

2. As you open the door, what is your very first impression? This will often be triggered by a sense, such as smell, sight, sound, etc. How does this sensation make you feel?

3. Continue to look around and build on your impressions: how does the space look? For example, is it clean or dusty, minimalist or cluttered? There are no right or wrong impressions, and this isn't about casting judgements on your housekeeping skills – you are simply observing what is around you.

4. How does the space around you make you *feel*? Do you feel comfortable and relaxed or stressed from all the things around you calling to be dealt with – like a visual To-Do list?

5. What could you do to make this space feel better? Is it simply a case of tidying, decluttering and cleaning, moving furniture around, sourcing

more appropriate storage systems, or adding some personal touches like photos, flowers and plants to soften the space?

6. If you could only own five possessions for the rest of your life, what would they be? Pondering this question will help you release what material possessions have importance in your life, and how they integrate with your home. For example, I love my piano and like to position it in the heart of our home, so it is easily accessible and visible – this also helps me remember to play it.

TLC (aka Tender Loving Cleaning)

I have a love-hate relationship with cleaning. I love the feeling of having a clean house, and I actually enjoy the activity of cleaning – the physical movement, as well as the satisfaction of seeing an area transformed 'before and after'. I don't enjoy how frequently cleaning needs to be done; where *does* all that dust come from? I also seem to be the only one who does the cleaning in our house, which I protest about loudly and regularly, even though it falls on deaf ears.

Facing a few hectic weeks at work recently, I conceded that the only way I would be able to cope with the housework was with the assistance of a cleaner. It's taken me a long time to see the value of getting a cleaner. Having a cleaner always seemed like a luxury reserved for high-income earners. My perception of having a cleaner has also been influenced by my childhood when I watched my hard-working parents run their accommodation business. For many years, they cleaned all the units and washed the linen themselves – until they realised their efforts would be better focused on working *on* their business rather than in their business.

Even when they sold their business and were both working full time, Saturday was still our cleaning day at home. Even though there were only three of us living in our household, and the mess was limited, the secret to success was keeping on top of it every week by scheduling time scheduled in to make it happen. Friday afternoon was reserved for grocery shopping, and Saturday morning was cleaning time, which included tidying, vacuuming and mopping, as well as cleaning the bathrooms. Everyone had a job to do, and we just got on and did it. My parents introduced me to cleaning at a young age – I still vividly remember cleaning the bathroom as an eight-year-old.

Fast-forward a few decades, and I recognise how busy life is compared to when I was growing up. In addition to work and school, the kids have after school activities most afternoons, and weekends are usually consumed with birthday parties and playdates or other DIY jobs around the house and in the garden. We are responsible for creating this busy lifestyle, and it seems to be the way of life for most families these days. Realising and accepting how different life is now, compared to how it was when I was growing up, was when I finally decided it was time to let go of the housework (at least on this occasion) and reach out for help.

A friend recommended a cleaner who I organised to come around to our house and prepare a quote. She remarked on the amount of work required and recommended adding extra time to her standard 3 hours. Ouch! It wasn't *that* bad, was it? While the total cost was more than I was expecting, the feeling of walking into a sparkling-clean house that evening was worth every cent! The cleaner offered to come back every fortnight, which sadly I couldn't justify financially, but I certainly see the value in paying for a deep clean every few months.

The advantage of a deeper clean or spring clean is that it frees up more time for me to focus on other household tasks, such as decluttering and re-organising draws and cupboards, which quickly get out of control with multiple people putting things back in the wrong place. I have learnt as soon as the storage spaces are neglected, the clutter starts breeding in other places. If I can keep the draws and cupboards in order, there is enough space for things to go back where they belong, rather than being abandoned on the bench or dining table. Gretchen Rubin sums it up in her book, *The Happiness Project*, when she writes: "One of life's small pleasures is to return something to its proper place".

The deeper clean also lasted a few weeks, and I find that when the house is 'reset' to a certain level of cleanliness, everyone in the household tries to keep it that way for as long as possible. It's not until we have a super busy week and everyone is running low on energy that it slips again; in which case I could probably justify another visit from the cleaner.

If a cleaner is not an option, I would highly recommend investing in good quality cleaning appliances or the right appliance for the job. For years we had the same small unbranded vacuum cleaner, which did a good job in our small apartment. However, it quickly died when we moved into a larger house. When considering other options to replace it, we decided that although expensive, a Dyson seemed like the best choice. Everyone we knew who had one loved them, and they seemed to last forever. We selected our model and waited until one of the electrical stores ran a special offer, and we snapped one up. It is still going strong more than five years later.

The other cleaning appliance worth its weight in gold is my carpet shampooer. I purchased the $99 entry price point model to clean our rugs. We have wooden floors throughout, so the kids gravitate to the soft rugs to play Lego and other games, and the rugs pick up their fair share of dirt and grime. I clean the rugs a couple of times a year and am astounded, as well as a little disgusted, by the colour of the water that comes out of them after cleaning. I hang the clean, damp rugs over our fence on a hot day, and they're dry by the afternoon. There are more expensive models which claim to 'dry carpets immediately after washing', but this model is all I need to revitalise my rugs.

Love Lessons:

1. Consider the areas in your home that need TLC (Tender Loving Cleaning). How likely are you to ever get to these areas, and how much will it

bother you if you don't? Would the relief of getting these jobs done outweigh the cost of a cleaner?

2. Make a list of jobs that need doing, especially the ones not done regularly, such cleaning windows and windowsills, skirting boards, deep-cleaning the fridge and oven and cooktop, decluttering, etc. Schedule a time to do these jobs one weekend, or break them down over a few weekends. Alternatively, book a cleaner specifically for these tasks.

3. A-draw-a-day. Some people like to have an epic declutter every year. The advantage of this method is that it gets the job done, and you don't need to think about it (or dread it) for another year. However, I personally find this method very overwhelming – the mess always gets worse before it gets better when decluttering this way. There is also no way I can sit and go through things methodically without 'help' from the kids.

Bite-size decluttering is my preferred strategy – one draw or cupboard at a time. By the time I work my way around the house, it's usually time to start again, but in the interim, I know what's in each draw. For me, the main benefit of going through draws with the intention of decluttering is finding stuff you forgot you had. Some of this can be tossed, but I have so many 'Christmas Day moments' when I discover things I love but have completely forgotten about. I aspire to a minimalistic house, but I am also a creative person and love being surrounded by colour and inspiring things. I'm at peace with being a bower bird if I continue to use and appreciate the things I collect.

4. Invest in appliances and cleaning equipment to make cleaning easier and more pleasant. Think about the jobs you hate doing or that frustrate you. Would the right tool for the job or a better quality one make this task quicker and easier?

All the Small Things

As with many areas in life, it's the small things that make the biggest difference – that stunning pair of earrings to complete an outfit, flowers on a table, or a kind gesture. In the same way, it's the little things that make our houses homes. This year, a couple of carefully chosen items have really enhanced my relationship with our home.

Since I was a small child, I have longed to name a house or a property. One day I was tidying my children's rooms and dusting around the name plaques they were given as babies. These name plaques are exquisite. Each name is hand-painted in vibrant colours and includes a unique image next to the name; an owl for my daughter and a digger for my son. I picked one up to admire it, flipped it over and noticed a sticker with the contact details of the little company that makes them. Intrigued, later that day I looked up the web address and was pleasantly surprised to learn that in addition to children's names, they also did house name plaques. The seed was planted, and I started to imagine what we could call our house.

I drew inspiration for our house name from our location and surroundings. Our house is positioned in the middle of a large suburban block in a fringe suburb. As a result, there are a lot of established trees and an abundance of wildlife in our neighbourhood. I am particularly fond of the established gums that encircle our home.

Sitting in our garden one day, the iconic Aussie song, *Home Among the Gumtrees* by John Williamson, popped into my head. Reflecting on the first line of lyrics, about a home among the gumtrees and plum trees, I smiled to myself as I mentally checked off the gumtrees *and* plum trees growing on our property. I toyed with the words in my head until 'Among the Gumtrees' stuck. With a slight modification, I settled on 'Among the Gums'. After checking in with my family, it *is* their house too; I placed the order for our house name with the same company that had produced our children's plaques. They were absolutely wonderful to work with on a custom order and were very helpful in determining which colour combinations would stand out *and* complement our house.

We receive so many compliments on our beautiful house name plaque. I feel it has personified our house by attaching more emotion to it. When you name anything from a car to a boat or even a pet, a bond is established between you and the object. It's like adding a little bit of your soul to something you cherish.

I always marvelled at how 'visible' the wind is around our house, compared to our previous house, which was in a new suburb without many trees. Even the slightest breath of wind is visible in the movement of the leaves on the trees. If the wind grows stronger, we can see each tree move differently with the rhythm of the wind, like lunges contracting and expanding. The movement and sound of the wind has always fascinated me and reminds me of the wind chimes we had in my childhood home. For me, the sound of wind chimes conjures many nostalgic memories – something I thought would be special to recreate for my children.

The hunt for wind chimes began. Wind chimes are not the type of item that can be purchased online. The sounds they make vary greatly and need to resonate with the listener. For the best part of the year, I scoured every gift shop I came across for wind chimes. While I found plenty of wind chimes that *looked* great, their sound didn't meet my expectations. The sound was my priority. I was seeking a harmonious collection of notes with a deep, resonating timbre. Sounds easy, right? Wrong! Most chimes were too high-pitched and tinny, not a pleasant sound at all.

I finally found the perfect set of chimes in a gift shop on the NSW South Coast. They are a medium-sized set with a beautiful tone. They consist of metal tubes and a wooden clapper, yes, that's what it's called! The wooden clapper is the key; it creates a softer, melodic sound that is more natural than metal on metal.

I hung our wind chimes outside our kitchen window, and I now relish windy days. The gentle jingle of these chimes has enhanced my awareness of nature. I now *hear* the difference between a gentle breeze and a robust gust of wind as I live more mindfully in tune with nature's rhythms.

"A house is made of bricks and beams. A home is made of hopes and dreams."

– UNKNOWN

• CHAPTER 9 •

The Natural World

"The best remedy for those who are frightened, lonely or unhappy is to go outside, somewhere they can be alone, alone with the sky, nature and God. For then and only then can you feel that everything is as it should be and that God wants people to be happy amid nature's beauty and simplicity. I firmly believe nature can bring comfort to all who suffer."

– ANNE FRANK

Memories of Nature

In *The Healing Magic of Forest Bathing*, author Julia Plevin captures the importance of love in all relationships we have. Not just with other people, but with ourselves and Earth, when she writes, "In a reinforcing loop, the more we love ourselves, the more we love the earth, and the more we love one another. Simply put, loving energy has the power to transform the world. It may sound a bit hippie-dippie until you understand the quantum physics. Positive emotions and operating from a place of love and peace within yourself results in your body emitting different electromagnetic frequencies that can change your experience of reality as well as the experience of those around you."

I have had a close affinity with nature for as long as I can remember. My mental and physical well-being depends on me spending as much time in nature as possible. I can still clearly recall one of my first memorable experiences with nature. We had two large water tanks in our backyard on Norfolk Island. They were completely necessary to capture the rainwater we needed for our water supply before we sunk a bore, but regardless of what colour dad painted them, they were ugly.

Mum thought planting a little garden bed around the edge of the tanks would soften and distract from their overwhelming presence. I was about four at the time, and she enlisted my help to plant out the garden. She had selected a white miniature rose and marigolds that would be grown from seed. The rose was tiny, and I marvelled at how plants would grow from the tiny slivers that mum said were the marigold seeds. We planted, we watered, and we waited. Thanks to Norfolk's mild, humid climate, it wasn't long before the little seedlings sprung from the soil, vivid green shoots reaching for the sun. The rose didn't take long to settle either, and once established, was swathed with creamy-white blossoms for more time than it wasn't. I remember checking the progress of these little plants every day, marvelling at their willingness to grow so freely.

From that point I was hooked. I couldn't get enough of plants and seeds and was eager to learn how to grow more. My parents showed me how to strike cuttings from plants, which they probably regretted as I filled our back porch with pots containing an assortment of experimental cuttings. An assortment of begonias, camellias, Bloodleaf (Iresine herbstii), geraniums, daisies, ferns, and anything else I could get my hands on. Most were successful and before I knew it, I had more plants than I knew what to do with. We managed to plant quite a few around our property and gave the rest to friends.

As a kid in the 80 and 90s, I was fortunate to grow up with the television program Gardening Australia. This further fuelled my enthusiasm for gardening, inspiring new projects and ideas and helped me learn the names of countless plants. One year our Guide group entered their Scarecrow competition, and we received a mention on the show.

As I grew older, I looked for every opportunity to spend time outside. I was fortunate to grow up on a 7-acre property on Norfolk Island, which provided me with all the space I needed to build cubbies, create imaginary worlds, wander, and dream. We had a valley with a veggie patch at the bottom, lush, wild forests brimming with birds, as well as traditional garden beds. My parents both enjoyed gardening. However, it was somewhat of a necessity to grow our own fresh fruit and vegetables, which we couldn't always buy from the local shops due to strict Island quarantine and the frequency of the supply ship. As challenging as this could sometimes be, there's nothing I would change about growing up in this enriching environment.

Love Lessons:

1. Think back to your childhood and your first memorable experience in nature. For many people, this is a positive experience that evokes happy memories. How can you recreate this experience in your adult life? For me, this is planting seeds and striking cuttings – anything that creates new life in my garden. For others, this could be skimming stones in a creek, going on a bushwalk, or visiting a

special natural place you enjoyed visiting as a child. By recreating these experiences in adulthood, we reinforce our love for and bond with nature.

2. Mother Teresa once said, "Love is a fruit in season at all times, and within reach of every hand." There's nothing sweeter or nutritious than in-season fruit and vegetables.

Make a list of your favourite fruits and vegetables. Enjoy more of these in your current life by:

Growing them yourself.

Visiting a local farmer's market to source them.

Swapping produce with friends.

Planning a trip to visit a region that specialises in fresh produce, especially when they host a regional food festival, such as the National Cherry Festival in Young, NSW, or the Batlow CiderFest.

3. Gaze into a flower. When was the last time you looked, *really* looked at a flower? Stand still and mindfully stare into a flower, taking in its colours, petals, sepals, stamens, stigma, anthers, etc. A flower comprises so many parts – it is almost like looking into another world. As Buddha wisely said, "If we could see the miracle of a single flower

clearly, our whole life would change." I have no doubt this is true.

On a trip to Japan a few years ago, we were walking along a grand parade on a balmy late summer evening when the scent struck me. Rosemary. I was instantly transported back to my grandma's garden in Australia, where we often sat on her front verandah on a warm summer evening like this, inhaling the earthy scent of rosemary mingled with dry eucalyptus. The aroma of rosemary is distinctive, and the oil is often used in aromatherapy for enhancing memory and concentration. I was astounded that despite being thousands of kilometres away in a completely different country and culture, my memories were instant and vivid. Nature can effortlessly stimulate all of our senses: scent, sight, sound, taste, and touch, which can awaken the deepest memories. This is how powerfully entwined we are with nature.

The Gift of Nature

One of the best treats I received this year was a family pass to a local tulip garden with a spectacular display of tulips and other spring-flowering bulbs and plants throughout September and October every year. This was a very special gift, as it was given to me for the voluntary work I had done in the garden outside the childcare centre my children go to. This tulip garden is also one of my favourite gardens that I genuinely look forward to going to every year. You can easily lose hours in this garden; there is enough space to set up a picnic and for the kids to run around without disturbing other visitors.

I went there with my son at the end of September. I should have been at home working as I had several deadlines, but the weather was so beautiful I couldn't resist. My son came out with some hilarious comments such as, "Mum, I don't like flowers, but this garden is wonderful!". He assessed the garden beds and selected his favourite flowers, and we enjoyed a sausage sandwich and chips on the picnic blanket under the bowers of flowering trees. There were no toys, TV, or other distractions – it was a magical experience.

I have enjoyed giving plants as Christmas gifts over the last few years. I try to select bullet-proof plants, such as African Daisies, geraniums, and succulents. I start planning these gifts in spring to ensure I have enough to give to friends, my children's teachers, neighbours, as well as my book club group, which is probably over thirty plants. However, I get such a sense of satisfaction from propagating these plants and passing them onto homes where they will grow for years in the recipients' gardens.

My recipients are always thrilled to receive a plant as a gift. Giving someone a living gift is very touching – for the giver and the receiver. You are entrusting them with the life of another living thing, such a special responsibility. One of the most beautiful moments I have experienced when gifting a plant was the reaction I received from my daughter's teacher. We were all rushing as the morning bell rang on the last day of school, so I quickly thrust a plant at her as she was closing the classroom door to start the day. As she took the plant in her hands, she stopped in her tracks, spellbound. Her eyes glazed over, and she smiled as she nostalgically recalled how the smell of the geranium reminded her of her grandmother. In an instant, amidst the chaos of the last day of school, the fragrance of this tiny plant transported her somewhere wonderful. *This* is the joy of plants.

Grow a Garden

Anyone can enjoy the benefits of a garden and growing plants. Regardless of how little space you have, you can still grow plants in pots indoors, on a balcony, or in a courtyard. The key is quality over quantity. Anytime spent with plants is better than none.

There are many important life lessons to be learnt from gardening, such as patience and consistency. Landscape designer and author Michael Bates believes, "It's about being in the moment". Bates views gardening as a journey, saying,

"Because gardening's done over time, when you're doing the gardening that you're doing now, you're observing the gardening that you did last week and the week before. Your good work is almost always rewarded – the longer you do it, the better you get." My experience with gardening is that your effort is directly proportional to the reward, and seeing the fruits of your labour, quite literally, is incredibly encouraging and gratifying.

Everyone's reason for gardening will differ, and that's ok. Some people enjoy the satisfaction of growing their own produce; others love growing flowers they can pick and display in their home or create a low-maintenance native garden to attract local wildlife. "I grow neither flowers nor vegetables!" says Bates. "While it's deeply satisfying to grow your own food, the plant protection issues and pest management I find too troublesome. I'm a textural gardener – flowers come and go, but colour, form and texture composed artfully always look good. My wife grows some flowers, so I leave that to her."

I concur with Bates' wife and adore growing flowers. I love the simple satisfaction of picking something fresh from the garden to garnish or throw into a meal, and I'm equally as devastated when I discover my entire crop has been ravaged by possums or other veggie-hungry critters. In my experience, a lot of the flowering plants in my garden have been less vulnerable than their fruiting counterparts. I have great success with roses here in Canberra despite their temperamental reputation. The dry climate limits many of the fungal diseases they are susceptible to, and we seem to have enough ladybirds and praying mantises to combat aphids. The application of a slow-release fertiliser a couple of times a year results in an abundance of roses.

Find what you enjoy most about gardening and the types of plants that give you this satisfaction. "I like the glory gardening, where an hour of clipping fills a trailer and greatly transforms the space," says Bates. Some people love the order of lush green manicured hedges in a formal-style garden; others (like me) prefer the wild softness of a cottage-style garden. Simply find some plants you'd love to grow and go from there.

It is the process and consistent act of gardening, not the end goal that matters. Gardening symbolises something bigger than ourselves, Bates explains. "Gardens are life-affirming, good for the planet and a guilt-free pleasure. Your effort is always rewarded – now and later. It's one of the few virtuous cycles you can create in your life … it's the most fun you can have standing up!".

Forest Bathing

"Forget not that the earth delights to feel your bare feet and the wind longs to play with your hair."

– KAHLIL GIBRAN

A few years ago, I became aware of a Japanese practice known as Forest Bathing, or shinrin-yoku in Japanese. 'Shinrin' means forest in Japanese, and yoku means 'bath'. The intention of forest bathing is quite different to other activities. Whilst it is mindful, it is not meditation, nor is it a type of exercise, like walking or jogging. The purpose of forest bathing is to immerse all of your senses in the natural world, explains Qing Li in his article for www.time.com.

Research Li refers to in his article says that "By 2050, 66% of the world's population is projected to live in cities. According to a study sponsored by the Environmental Protection Agency, the average American spends 93% of his or her time indoors". These statistics are staggering and very sad. Many people in our world have lost their connection to nature, and this is severely impacting our mental and physical health.

"Researchers from the University of Essex found that in a group of people suffering from depression, 90 percent felt a higher level of self-esteem after a walk through a country park, and almost 75 percent felt less depressed. In another survey, the same research team found that 94 percent of people suffering from mental illness believed that contact with nature put them in a better mood," writes Julia Plevin in *The Healing Magic of Forest Bathing*.

Happily, Li believes anytime we spend in nature can be beneficial to reverse many of the negative health impacts of technology and busy, city-based lives. The act of forest bathing is quite simple, explains Li. Once you have found a natural spot, it is important to leave your phone and camera behind. The intent is to walk slowly, without any purpose of going anywhere specific, and letting your body guide you.

Li stresses that forest bathing is a personal activity. "There is no one-size-fits-all solution", and different people will prefer different environments, so it is important to go to places you are drawn to and feel comfortable in to get maximum benefit from your experience. In Japan, forest bathing is considered as such a personal experience that many forests offer personalised programs, guides and even doctors to assess bathers physically and psychologically prior to commencing the activity.

Forest bathing is an activity for the senses. Tune into the sights, sounds and smells around you and draw these in. Look as if you are looking at the natural world around you for the first time and wonder in its intricacies and magnificence. Notice things such as the sound of the wind through the leaves of the trees, birdsong, and other animal noises. Look at the colours of the earth, the trees, the sky, as well as how light plays on everything around you. Touch the surfaces around you – the trunk of a tree or other plants, rocks, leaves, anything you are drawn to. Touch is a very powerful way of connecting to the forest. Plevin recommends going a step further and *talking* to the trees you are drawn to. "Hold onto the tree and ask her a few questions, as though you're getting to know a new friend. Ask something as simple as, 'How are you?' or 'What's it like to be a tree?' Ask about her shape and life story: 'Why are you curved?' or 'What is your desire?' Often you'll receive an answer right away. Continue the conversation as long as it seems right. Ask the tree about your own life. Ask for advice or for help with a challenge or an upcoming decision. State your question in a complete sentence. Be clear. Ask the tree for more clarity on the answers she gives you. When the conversation feels complete, thank the tree for holding space, and give her an offering or a heartfelt prayer."

A number of different cultures also identify with Plevin's respect and personification of trees, perceiving trees as more than just large, long-lived plants. In his book, *The Song of Trees*, David George Haskell discusses this concept with Teresa Shiki, a Shuar woman, a healer, activist, and teacher who describes her relationship with the native forest: "Every tree is a living person, with speech. Ceibo represents all plant life; you cannot listen to 'one' tree; there is no one tree living alone ... Our dreams are attached to the roots of plants, big and small, and to our ancestors." In Shiki's culture, trees are revered and accepted as their own entities with unique personalities. In addition to this, the trees are connected not only to each other but also to the world around them in the past, present and future.

Taste and smell are also an incredibly important part of the forest bathing experience. Inhale and taste the air around you. What does it smell and taste like? As you inhale and taste the air, you are inhaling phytoncides – this is the science bit. As a child who grew up roaming through pine forests, this all makes complete sense, and something I'm sure we *all* know intuitively; now, there's science to prove it.

Plevin explains there are two components believed to be responsible for the healing benefits of forest bathing: phytoncides and negative ions. Add soil microbes to these other elements and you have a healing trifecta. This is how it works, writes Plevin: "Phytoncides are produced to help plants and trees protect themselves from harmful insects and germs; in the process, they help us in similar ways. Negative ions are tiny molecules produced in nature that offer mood-enhancing benefits. When we forest bathe, we breathe in phytoncides, negative ions, and soil bacteria; together, they provide health benefits. These tiny particles work wonders even when we're not aware of them, but forest bathing with the intention of healing magnifies their effects."

Let's consider these elements in more detail:

Negative Ions
The more we learn about the world around us, the more we realise how it's often the things we can't see with the naked eye that have the biggest impact. This is certainly the case with negative ions, which happily exist everywhere in nature. Negative ions have a unique reaction within our body to increase our well-being. This is the process, explains Plevin: "Negative ions are invisible molecules found in the forest, the mountains, and near water, such as oceans and waterfalls. When you visit these places, you absorb the negative ions into your bloodstream, which produces a biochemical reaction that boosts production of serotonin, the neurotransmitter that's responsible to alleviating depression and relieving stress. The negatively ionized air promotes alpha brain waves and increases brain wave amplitude, creating an overall clear and

calming effect. In other words, exposure to negative ions leads to good vibes."

Soil Bacteria
Growing up on Norfolk Island, I was surrounded by rich volcanic soil, which has instilled in me the love of organic, aromatic earth. There's nothing more grounding than plunging your hands into freshly cultivated soil to sow a crop. Soil also plays an important role in the forest and in our well-being. In the same way, negative ions interact with our serotonin, so too does soil bacteria, "The healing powers of nature are abundant in the forest air and floor. A cure to distress can also be found in a handful of forest soil. Exposure to the soil bacteria, *Mycobacterium vaccae* can improve our immune health and emotional health by acting as a natural antidepressant that increases the release and metabolism of serotonin in parts of the brain that control cognitive function," explains Plevin.

Forest Bathing is just the tip of the iceberg when it comes to our immersion in nature. Florence Williams identifies the importance of daily access to green space in her book, *The Nature Fix: Why Nature Makes Us Happier, Healthier, and More Creative:* "we all need nearby nature: we benefit cognitively and psychologically from having trees, bodies of water and green spaces just to look at; we should be smarter about landscaping our schools, hospitals, workplaces and neighborhoods so everyone gains. We need quick incursions to natural areas that engage our senses. Everyone needs access to clean, quiet and safe natural refuges in a city".

Williams also notes that any connection with nature – no matter how brief – is beneficial, but the longer, the better. "Short exposures to nature can make us less aggressive, more creative, more civic-minded and healthier overall. For warding off depression, let's go with the Finnish recommendation of five hours a month in nature, minimum. But as the poets, neuroscientists and river runners have shown us, we also at times need longer, deeper immersions into wild spaces to recover from severe distress, to imagine our futures and to be our best civilized selves."

Put Your Trust in the Earth

Many of us live hectic lives comprised of complex decisions and monumental problems. However, spending time in nature provides perspective and melts away many of these problems, so the monumental soon seems trivial. Plevin believes that we should share our problems with nature, using nature like a cradle of comfort to alleviate our fears. I particularly love this technique she shares: "If you're feeling overwhelmed with life, simply lie down on the earth. Allow the weight of your body to sink into the ground and feel the sense that you are being held. Surrender your whole being. A fern doesn't worry about how it's going to unfurl. Be like the fern and know you are supported. Stay there in Nature's cradle until you're ready to continue".

Portals are another technique Plevin uses to incite transformation. For many, the powerful visualisation and sensation of walking under or through something can inspire change. Plevin suggests to "Look for a portal along the trail – an arched branch or some other natural doorway that you can walk through. When you walk through this portal, you'll be in a new dimension where your dreams are already real."

Love Lessons:

1. The next time you are facing a problem, go for a walk in nature. If you're feeling particularly troubled, find somewhere quiet and secluded to lie down and surrender to the earth, releasing any negative emotions. Notice how you feel before your walk, then afterwards. Record your experience in a journal so you can reflect on it later.

2. Take a journal with you on your walk and take some time to record your thoughts, fears, hopes, and dreams. Contemplating these things in nature will give you some perspective and, hopefully, some inspiration.

3. Portals – Find a portal (an arched branch, for example) on your next forest walk. Before you proceed through the portal, identify the things in your life you want to let go of, such as fear, anxiety,

or toxic people. As you proceed through your portal, visualise these negative influences in your life melting away and dissipating back into the universe. They are not yours to hold onto. Trust that nature can absorb all that is no longer serving you. Once you have reached the other side of the portal, observe how light you feel now you are no longer carrying these burdens.

Find your Rhythm

Our ancestors used to move in time with nature – they would rise with the sun and retire when the sun set. Technology has allowed us to flick a light on whenever we want and often means we're awake late into the night, watching TV, or on devices. This convenience has allowed us to cram more into our already busy days, but at what cost? We are out of step with nature, as well as our bodies, by ignoring our circadian rhythms. Natural rhythms are important, explains Plevin: "Everything in nature has a rhythm; it's how the planet keeps track of time. Each day has a rhythm.

Seasons have a rhythm, as do moon cycles, ocean tides, river currents and weather patterns. Spring is for making new plans and sowing seeds. Summer is for working hard, staying out late, and celebrating. Fall is for harvesting the fruits of your labors and storing them for winter. Winter is a time to slow down and go internal. Each season prepares us for the next. When we align our lives to the flow of nature, we're able to move with grace. Your body is an instrument of the earth, but it might be out of tune. You can tune yourself as you would a guitar to harmonize with all of life."

Love Lessons:

1. Think about your current daily rhythm or routine. What time do you rise and go to bed, eat meals, work, exercise, and relax? How well do you sleep? Could your life be improved by having a more consistent rhythm?

2. Now, consider your seasonal rhythm. Does your routine change much between summer and winter, for example? What seasonal rhythms could

you capitalise on during these seasons? For example, rising early to go for a run, or taking a walk after dinner during summer, and spending time reading or studying on cold winter evenings.

3. Organise your goals and plans for the year ahead to align with the best time of year to do them. For example, committing to a morning run in the middle of winter could be setting yourself up for failure when you could go during the warmer part of the day. I love walking my dog at first light during summer. However, first light during Canberra winter is often accompanied by sub-zero temperatures, so during the colder months, I walk him later in the morning or early afternoon.

4. The seasons can also influence when you choose to rest throughout the year. Pick the time of year you feel the flattest and book a holiday somewhere invigorating to recharge.

Time is a key part of our natural rhythms and can be perceived or utilised in different ways. "The Greeks had two words for time – *chronos* and *kairos*," says Plevin. "*Chronos* refers to minutes and seconds – it's the time displayed on our phone screens. *Kairos* is the opportune moment – it's the *right timing*. See what happens when you shift into your own sense of *kairos*. Find your own beat as you move through the forest." Finding our 'own beat' is also important as we navigate our way through life, one day, month, season, and year, at a time.

Grounding

I love Plevin's take on the benefits of 'grounding' in *The Healing Magic of Forest Bathing*, as she writes: "The earth is the greatest source of energy available to us. Our planet is like one huge battery that is constantly being recharged from solar radiation and lighting from above as well as from its deep-down molten core. When you walk barefoot, you absorb free electrons into your body, neutralizing and releasing toxic free radicals. The two hundred thousand nerve endings on the sole of each foot pick up the electrons transferred from the earth. Walking barefoot will calm your nervous system and help your body return to an optimal electrical state, from which you're better able to self-regulate and self-heal."

In her book, *Phosphorescence*, Julia Baird also shares her own healing experience, derived from the grounding benefits of nature, as she recalls, "In my own quest to become phosphorescent, in which I lost myself many times in dark holes and swamps, it was awe and wonder I kept returning to, and the quiet healing properties of nature – of forests, the sea, and the creatures they contain. So many of us have our quiet places of escape and refuge. Nearby beaches, a park bench, a magnificent tree."

Love Lessons:

Grounding Techniques:

In her book, there is an activity Plevin shares called *walking tree breaths*, which she learnt from a Shamanic Reiki teacher and author, Llyn Cedar Roberts. This is an excellent exercise to do when you're feeling disconnected and need to ground yourself. Many guided meditations ask you to visualise roots going from your feet into the earth, but this practice becomes more powerful if you can do it outside and incorporate the breathing technique as follows:

1. Take off your shoes and, while standing, rock back and forth and side to side to establish a firm connection to the earth. Imagine that roots are attached to the bottoms of your feet that extend down deep into the ground.

2. Inhale deeply and imagine energy travelling through your feet, up your legs, through your core, and into your heart centre.

3. Exhale as you reach your arms to the sky like branches reaching for the light and let out a "shooo!" sound as you expel energy that's been stuck in your body.

4. On your next inhale, gather energy from the cosmos and bring it into your heart centre.

5. Exhale as you fold forward and let out another "shooo!" as you bring your fingertips to the ground. It's okay to bend your knees. Allow your fingertips to soak up the energy from the earth.

6. As you stand, inhale and bring your hands to your heart centre in a prayer position. Repeat six to twelve times.

In addition to the feet, grounding can also be done through other parts of the body.

Plevin describes another traditional practice she was introduced to, called the Siberian Mark, whereby you rest your forehead on the ground, thereby 'grounding' your third eye. This is a particularly powerful way to enhance your connection with the earth and may result in a vision or intuition.

1. Spread out a blanket, or lie directly on the ground if you can find a soft, safe space.

2. Start on your hands and knees, then come down onto your shins and rest your forehead on the ground, so you are in the yoga position known as Child's Pose. You can keep your knees together or apart and put your hands straight above your head or by your side. The key is keeping your forehead in connection with the earth.

Relax and remain in this position for as long as your body needs. You may receive a vision, or you may not. The key is to make a deep connection to the earth.

The Joy of Sunrise

"The simple things are also the most extraordinary things, and only the wise can see them."

— PAULO COELHO, THE ALCHEMIST

On the last day of our holiday on Norfolk Island, I awoke before dawn and drove down to Emily Bay, a gorgeous little swimming bay protected from waves by a reef. The edges of the bay are softened with vibrant green grass and Norfolk Island pine trees – it's picture-postcard perfect. Parking the car, I walked to the Point and then along the beach as the sun rose. I pretty much had the place to myself, and this quiet time watching the sun rise over the ocean allowed me to connect with my surroundings and fully immerse myself in the experience. Watching the sun rise is a simple activity I try to do as often as possible – it is grounding and revitalising. Sunrise is a sacred time, reconnecting us to the awe-inspiring beauty of nature surrounding us every day, that we often fail to notice.

Take a Nature Break

"No matter where you are, you can always return home to Nature. You are rooted here."

– JULIA PLEVIN, THE HEALING MAGIC OF FOREST BATHING

At Easter, we were fortunate to be invited on a group holiday with our neighbours to a historic cottage in the Kosciusko National Park. The settlement consists of three separate buildings guests can stay in, depending on the size of the party. The cottage we stayed in had a rustic, pioneer style, indicative of the late 1800s, and was formerly used for accommodating farm workers.

I have been fortunate to travel to many beautiful places in my life, but none quite like this. There's soothing comfort in being so close to nature – watching the wild brumbies and kangaroos graze around our cottage – as well as staying in such a magnificent time-worn cottage. The cottage is permeated with the smell of old wood and smoke from thousands of fires in the well-worn stone fireplace. Despite its rustic appearance, the interior has a warm cosiness, akin to being embraced in a wooden womb. There's something magical about this enchanting place, surrounded by ancient Snow Gums and pristine alpine skies. Walking tracks traverse the plains and forests, but we were content to wander the surrounding moorlands within cooee and eyesight of our cottage.

With no mobile reception or electricity, apart from some solar panels to power the fridge, 'screen-time' doesn't exist here. Children need to be resourceful to make their own entertainment and fun. Fortunately for our kids, a large pile of rocks had been deposited at the front of the cottage to be compacted into a parking area in front of the building. But the kids didn't see rocks – they saw the materials required to build a fairy village. Over the course of five days, the kids transformed several meters square into 'Fairyland'. Each child was assigned a role, such as the architect of the houses, engineer for the roads and landscaper, to make the resulting project more efficient. Hours were spent each day building and refining this enchanted city. The adults marvelled at how effortlessly they forgot TV, iPads, and the creature comforts of home, relishing in the primeval pleasures of playing with dirt, rocks, and sticks. They transformed into children mindfully immersed in nature's toys.

As we made our way home along the winding gravel road, our hearts sank a little every time we saw evidence of civilisation – road signs, sealed roads, and finally, shops and houses. Our phones chimed simultaneously with notifications as we located mobile reception just out of Adaminaby. But there was an absence of that manic urge to devour messages and emails with the same fervour as five days before. Whilst we were glad to arrive back to the comfort and warmth of our home, a longing for this simplified existence lingered – so much so, within weeks I had booked another break there in

December. Our December trip was equally as restorative as the first, so I'm confident this will be a regular destination.

In October, we took a two-week break to drive up to the Sunshine Coast via Coffs Harbour to spend time with family and friends. I was very sad to leave my garden, as spring is such a beautiful time in Canberra. I also feared all my hard work in the garden prior to our trip would be in vain, with everything drying out and dying while we were away.

A few days before we departed, I learnt of a plant fair at Kariong on the NSW Central Coast, which was the perfect spot to stop to break up our journey. We stopped for an hour and a half over lunchtime, and I enjoyed wandering to look at the plants – the rest of the family not so much, but they all enjoyed the break and sausage sandwiches.

In Coffs Harbour the next day, we found ourselves at the Botanic Gardens, which were truly spectacular. The gardens were landscaped in an organic way, following the contours of the land along a path meandering through diverse landscapes, from lush tropical rainforest to native mangroves, formal English-style rose gardens, a Japanese Zen garden overlooking a lake, and riverside native bushland.

Love Lessons:

1. Incorporate nature breaks into your next holiday

Taking a break in nature can be refreshing when travelling, especially if you are covering long distances in a car or on a plane. It's a relief to stretch your legs after a few hours in the car or taking a long flight, so stopping somewhere where you can walk is much more refreshing than a servo stop. The next time you plan a trip – even if it is just a weekend break with family, check out any natural scenic spots along the way or at your destination and plan your breaks accordingly. Even if you still need to get fuel or food, minimise these stops and get takeaway so you can spend longer at your nature stop.

2. Plan your holiday around a natural attraction

The next time you book a holiday, consider alternatives to a city break. For example, rather than staying in Melbourne, you could stay along any of the picturesque coastlines around Port Phillip Bay or just outside Melbourne in the Dandenong Ranges. You are close enough to allow a day trip to the Big Smoke but faraway enough to detox in nature. If you have to stay in a city like Melbourne, for example, check out the natural sites within the city, such as the Botanical Gardens, which has a fantastic children's garden, or Fitzroy and Carlton Gardens.

3. Meet family and friends in nature

Instead of, or, as well as visiting family and friends, arrange to meet them in relaxing, natural settings. Many caravan parks are located close to beaches, rivers, and forests, serving as the perfect setting for catching up for a weekend or longer. Most parks also have self-contained cabins if you're not into roughing it too much.

COURTNEY SYMES

Placing Hope in Nature

"The creation of a thousand forests is in one acorn."

– RALPH WALDO EMERSON

One of the most reassuring things about nature is how quickly it recovers from adversity. This resilience instils a sense of hope, which is motivating when we're struggling in life, for whatever reason. If we look to nature as a source of inspiration during tough times and observe how she fights to survive, hopefully, this will offer us the strength to carry on.

When we first moved to our suburb, there was a house in our neighbourhood with a slightly neglected front yard, including some standard roses, which hadn't been shown any TLC for a very long time. Knowing how expensive standard roses are, this troubled me so much I often thought about sneaking into the front yard of this property one night and sprinkling a bit of fertiliser and water around the base of these roses. They were in such poor health I didn't even know what colour they were, as they had never flowered. Roses can be pretty tough, but they'll never reward you with flowers if you don't feed them.

Fast-forward a few years, and the house with the roses was sold. The new owners were clearly more into gardening than the previous owners. As soon as they moved in, they started to focus their attention on the garden. Within weeks the roses had been watered and mulched and happily yielded vibrant yellow blooms. This filled my heart with joy, reinforcing my belief in nature's determination to survive the toughest conditions, as well as thrive when shown love.

On a trip to the South Coast of NSW, around 12 weeks after the devastating summer bushfires had ravaged many of the quaint, small villages, we took a weekend break to celebrate our wedding anniversary and support the local communities there.

As we drove along the Kings Highway, which had understandably been closed for weeks so trees and debris could be removed, and infrastructure repaired, we were astounded by the amount of vegetative regrowth in the forests bordering the road. The kids kept asking where the bushfire had gone, and we kept telling them that it would have engulfed the very road we were travelling on. Whilst we could still see the evidence of blackened trunks and charcoal on the ground, the regeneration far surpassed this, although I'm sure the animal populations will take longer to recover.

Regardless of the blow that strikes, nature continues to fight back. Bushfires and other natural disasters or regions impacted by nuclear disaster and subsequent radiation, such as Chernobyl and the Fukushima Prefecture, still demonstrate evidence of recovery, with many buildings, roads, and other infrastructure becoming overgrown. By putting our faith in nature, we can put faith in ourselves and mankind, knowing that life goes on – in some form or another – so we must never lose hope.

"Even if I knew that tomorrow the world would go to pieces, I would still plant my apple tree."

– MARTIN LUTHER

Love Lessons:

1. Short term

Plant something new in your garden today. Plant some bulbs, strike some cuttings, or sow some seeds. One of the best purchases I made this year was a mini greenhouse. It is essentially a 24-cell seed tray with a base and a clear plastic cloche with vents you can open and close to control moisture – all for under $10. Inspired by Erin Benzakein's book, *Floret Farm's Cut Flower Garden: Grow, Harvest, and Arrange Stunning Seasonal Blooms*, I purchased a selection of flower seeds to raise in my greenhouse with the intention of planting these in our veggie patch. I was fed up with the collection of local creatures eating the veggies and decided the best remedy would be colour in the form of flowers. Don't be constrained by planting certain things in certain places – plant veggies in your front yard or flowers in your veggie patch. Let your heart be your guide.

Research seeds that need to be sown next season and purchase these in advance. Store them in the order they need to be sown. I frequently find I have the wrong seeds for the wrong season. I put them back in the draw, only to forget to plant them when I need to. Putting a helpful reminder on your calendar, in your phone, or garden planner will also help!

2. Long term

Plant a tree or a plant that will live for a long time, such as a rose or grapevine. You could also bury a time capsule or something else special underneath it to leave a legacy for future generations. This is a fun activity to do with kids and helps them understand the concept of time.

Set long-term Nature Goals, such as natural places you'd like to visit (locally or overseas) or perhaps a trail you'd like to hike; improvements you'd like to do to your garden and natural space at home. Even if finances don't permit committing to anything yet, do the research and start planning.

Spending more time in nature doesn't need to be hard, expensive, or time-consuming. I love the simplicity of Florence Williams' coda from *The*

Nature Fix: Why Nature Makes Us Happier, Healthier, and More Creative:

> *"Go outside, often, sometimes in wild places. Bring friends or not. Breathe"*
>
> .

• CHAPTER 10 •

The Power Within

Finding meaning in meditation

*"Meditation is a divine gift.
Meditation simplifies our outer life and energises our inner life. Meditation gives us a natural and spontaneous life, a life that becomes so natural and spontaneous that we cannot breathe without being conscious of our own divinity."*

– SRI CHINMOY

Since I was a teenager, I've been aware of the concept of meditation when I'd get up early to do

Aerobics Oz Style in the lounge room and find my stepmother meditating on the couch. I'd stalk out of the room annoyed. The TV was in this room and there was enough space for me to jump around, but I didn't want to disturb her. I remember thinking, who wants to sit in a room in the dark doing nothing anyway? One day I asked her, "what do you think about when you sit there?" She responded, "nothing". Nothing?! How could anyone not *think*? It made about as much sense as a screen door on a submarine, and I couldn't understand it at all. When I said I didn't believe there was any way I could sit somewhere awake and not think, she explained that some people liked to focus on their breathing by counting breaths, or repeating a word or number over and over again, such as 'one'. By this point, she'd completely lost me. What was the *point*?

Fast-forward 20+ years, and I'm a mum juggling young children, work, and home life. Meditation persistently popped up in books and magazine articles I read, podcasts, and other media I was exposed to. With such a deep-rooted history in many cultures, I couldn't help but think there must be something in it. However, I found the practice of mediation overwhelming. It seemed there were so many ways to do it – guided meditation, transcendental meditation, walking meditation ... I didn't know where to start, so I didn't.

A friend then recommended the app Headspace, which I tried for a couple of weeks. I enjoyed their guided meditations, which were also short and achievable while the kids were napping. The only problem was that the content was limited unless you subscribed, and I couldn't justify the cost of a subscription at the time. Subscription-based apps are common, and many offer fantastic content and free trial periods, but I decided the simplicity of DIY meditation was more my style. I also didn't want to feel obliged to meditate because I was paying for it every month. This might be excellent motivation for some people, but I didn't need another 'thing' to feel guilty about if I couldn't do it as frequently as I'd hoped. I also discovered I like to listen to music when I meditate, although it's not essential, and I can still meditate if I don't have music.

One day I came across a brochure in a coffee shop promoting free evening meditation sessions at my local library. Free, local, *and* during the evenings when my husband was home? Count me in. The first session was on a cold June evening, and I worried I'd be the only one to turn up, but when I arrived, the room was packed with around a hundred people!

The 6-week course was run by the Canberra Sri Chinmoy Centre. I had heard of Sri Chinmoy before and had competed in several Sri Chinmoy fun runs in Melbourne and Canberra. The fun runs were usually smaller, community-run events and not as commercial as some of the larger sponsored fun runs, so I already had a positive feeling towards this organisation.

The course leader was a calm, gentle man who covered exactly what I wanted to know about meditation, such as: what it is, how it works, and the benefits. We also discussed the practicalities of meditation at home, like how long and how often, and where. With two small children these were all questions I sought answers to. At the time, I thought I'd have to postpone meditation until the kids were old enough to be quieter. These sound like crazy excuses now I look back on them but were valid concerns at the time.

The first class consisted of the definition of meditation, answers to FAQs, several breathing exercises, and a guided heart chakra meditation, which was really powerful. I left feeling like I was floating on a cloud – I was hooked!

A couple of points from the course really resonated with me:

1. The similarities between meditation and exercise – the more consistent you are, the better you will get, like exercising a muscle. Just like exercising though, you will also have some 'off-days'. Ironically, these are probably the days you need meditation the most, even when it is difficult. The important thing is to keep showing up.

2. We were encouraged to pick some inspiring words to assist connecting with our heart chakra. Examples included: peace, bliss, love, joy,

light, energy, gratitude, etc. I now use a combination of my own 'powerful' words as mantras when I meditate.

Over the six-week course, the number of people that attended each session declined every week. Initially, I couldn't understand it – the course material was excellent, and the leader and assistants were friendly and helpful. There was a table at the back of the room that had some of Sri Chinmoy's books and music for sale, but the intention of the course was not to sell merchandise. I suddenly had a flashback to my teenage self, and it struck me – meditation isn't for everyone. Or, more accurately, meditation won't help you until you are ready. As the saying goes, "when the student is ready, the teacher will appear." I was *finally* ready.

By the end of the course, I realised that meditation is a personal practice. It will differ from person to person, and this is how it should be. To continue the practice regularly, it needs to be done in a way that suits your lifestyle and personality.

The best advice I can offer is to try as many different types of meditation as you can. Read the books, research online, glean advice from others, do all the free trials or courses, then cancel or try something else if they don't work for you. The more you try, the more likely you'll find a style that resonates.

After the course, I meditated mid-afternoon while the kids were napping. I initially committed to ten minutes, as I was usually guaranteed no one would wake up during this time. I would set a timer on my phone, mostly so I didn't fall asleep myself, and sit on the couch in silence with my eyes closed. It is incredible how much energy ten minutes of sitting quietly can give you. For me, it was the equivalent of an afternoon nap without the grogginess when I woke up. I would usually allow myself five minutes after meditating just to sit and 'bring myself back'. Jumping up straight after meditating can be jarring and counterproductive.

I continue to mediate mid-afternoon, after I've allowed my lunch to settle. Now the kids are at school, I schedule my meditation session before school pick-up. This gives me an extra burst of energy to deal with their school's-out-craziness and helps me avoid the 3 pm 'slump' that drives most of us to coffee and chocolate.

The benefits of meditation are many and varied, but one that particularly appealed to me was the positive impact meditation has on sleep, which Arianna Huffington writes about in her book, *The Sleep Revolution: Transforming Your Life, One Night at a Time*, "Those who do contemplative retreats in hermitages are far from doing nothing, since they are constantly engaged in training their minds, but there is no 'noise,' no 'waste' to eliminate, no stress to cure, no chaos to reorganize. This means that there is less to repair during sleep and the sleep quality of meditators is deeper." It would seem that meditation is like a feather duster for the mind, and dusting regularly is favoured over an annual spring clean.

I usually meditate sitting on my bed, propped up with pillows, because I can close the door and feel comfortable in this space. However, my favourite place to meditate during the warmer months is in the beautiful hammock my husband bought me. I love the feeling of weightlessness the hammock provides – it allows me to drift – physically and mentally. There is also something magical about meditating outside, drawing the fresh air deeply into your lungs, and feeling the breeze tickle your skin.

Now my children are older, I often say to them, "Mummy's going to have some quiet relax time for fifteen minutes. Please play quietly and don't disturb me until I come out of the bedroom". Frequently, someone will come in 'starving', in urgent need of a snack, but for the most part they get it, and that's enough for me at the moment.

I recently experienced a beautiful moment with my son. Every day when we walk to school, he runs ahead, then sits on a fence and closes his eyes while he waits for us to catch up. Initially I thought he was trying to balance, which is more challenging with your eyes closed. When I asked him what he was doing, he replied, "I am trying to find peace. If I am calm, I do better in class." This completely floored me. I know the kids' school touches on mindfulness, yoga, and quiet time, but this seemed an unexpectedly sophisticated response for a six-year-old. Children are like little sponges – absorbing information from TV, the internet, friends, and family. I like to think their observation of my regular meditation practice has had a positive influence on them.

Love Lessons:

1. If you are new to meditation, check out free classes or groups in your local area. A beginner's class is an excellent introduction to understanding the benefits of meditation and building a foundation for your personal practice.

2. Check out online resources for meditation – there is an abundance of books, audiobooks, podcasts, apps, and YouTube videos. I personally love the Hay House podcast for free guided meditations and often accompany my meditation with music from the Peace or Meditation playlists on Spotify.

3. If you are ready to commence a regular meditation practice, consider how and when you could add this to your lifestyle. First thing in the

morning might not work for everyone, so meditate in your car, the park, a vacant meeting room during your lunch break, or in the evening before going to bed.

Seeking a Spiritually Guided Life

Over the last couple of years, it felt like I had been going around in circles. My life lacked focus and direction. So last year, in the hope of gaining some clarity around the path I should pursue in my crazy life, I contacted a psychic medium (recommended by a friend) for a reading. Unfortunately, the timing wasn't great for the medium, with a new baby due to arrive any day, so we agreed to get back in touch once her life with a new bub had settled down.

Several months went by, and because I had liked the medium's Facebook page, one day a post popped up in my feed. The post was about a spiritual weekend that the medium I had connected with was hosting with another medium. As I read the course description, my excitement piqued – it was like it was written for me. The course content covered the topics I was seeking clarity on, and I felt compelled to enrol, intuitively knowing this would be a special experience for me. So, after carefully considering the financial cost and a weekend away from my family and other commitments, I took a deep breath and enrolled.

The course, *Living a Spiritually Guided Life,* such an inspiring name, took place on a changeable spring weekend in September ... a metaphor for new beginnings, perhaps? The course content was all I could hope for and more, but one of the unexpected bonuses was meeting other like-minded students who had similar questions and challenges to me, even though we all came from a diverse range of backgrounds.

The weekend consisted of a number of exercises, such as defining personal boundaries, connecting with our inner child, embracing our Shadow Side, Soul Contracts, as well as work on our chakras, meditation, and an intense forgiveness exercise. Many of these concepts were new to me, even if I was familiar with their names.

For example, I had heard of chakras before (the complex energy system inside our body) but didn't realise there were more than seven, or what each energy centre was responsible for in our bodies and how to realign them. In addition, we did some chakra meditation, which enhanced my current daily practice.

We were also encouraged to bring our own crystals to work with over the weekend, which reignited a connection to my younger self. I had never 'worked' with crystals before but was aware that each crystal has different energy and healing properties.

My love of crystals, gemstones and rocks is a prime example of maintaining a connection with the things you loved doing as a child. I had an extensive rock collection as a kid, a passion inspired by my grandmother, who always had a beautiful collection of rocks and semi-precious stones proudly displayed in her lounge room. My grandmother loved the bush and lived in a region rich with sapphires, crystals, and other interesting rocks. We had regular bush picnics, where much of our time was spent wandering with our eyes cast to the ground, looking for the next interesting rock to add to our collections.

Over the years of clutter-clearing, I began to see my rock collection as a dust collector and sadly let go of many of the less precious pieces each time we moved house, even if they had sentimental value. It was joyful to reawaken this part of myself that had become suppressed over the years, especially since I hadn't recognised it was missing until now.

At the end of each day of the workshop I floated out of the room, feeling lighter and unburdened by my problems and the expectations of the external world. I wanted to experience this feeling again, so when we set our intentions at the end of the course, one of mine was 'to continue my spiritual journey'.

The word 'spiritual' is wonderfully fluid. I used to rigidly connect spirituality to religion, but I've since realised you can be a spiritual person, without identifying with any organised religious group. I now view religion as one of the many "pathways" to 'Spirit', and believe there is more than one path to the top of the mountain. I define 'Spirit' as everything around us, physical and non-physical, our connection to each other, nature and our environment, and the universe.

"It's not that the Universe was formed a long time ago and then suddenly stopped growing – it is continually expanding. And so are we."

– JULIA PLEVIN, THE HEALING MAGIC OF FOREST BATHING

During the times when we feel disconnected from the humans around us, I find comfort in believing we will always be connected to something greater than ourselves. This is also why I believe 'the breath' is so important in many meditation and mindfulness practices. This is our connection to life at the most basic level – it is something we and other plants and animals need to do to sustain life, and it is also done in a regular, steady rhythm. This is one thing all humans share, irrespective of age, gender, race, and social status, and the one thing we can keep doing when it feels like everything has gone to crap. Just keep breathing.

Love Lessons:

"A person who has achieved control over psychic energy and has invested it in consciously chosen goals cannot help but grow into a more complex being. By stretching skills, by reaching toward higher challenges, such a person becomes an increasingly extraordinary individual."

– MIHALY CSIKSZENTMIHALYI,
FLOW: THE PSYCHOLOGY OF OPTIMAL EXPERIENCE

1. Do you think of yourself as a spiritual person? What does spirituality mean to you? Write your answers in your journal to clarify your thoughts.
2. How can you reinvigorate your connection to Spirit or the Universe? Here are some ideas:
Instil a daily meditation practice

Go for a short walk in nature

Listen to inspiring, uplifting music

Seek out some new books or online videos from spiritual teachers who inspire you

Connect with others in a regular spiritual practice – this could be an organised religious group, a meditation class, or a course online or in-person

Attend a spiritual retreat – if you are short on time, this could just be for a day or a weekend. It's amazing how powerful a few hours of focusing on our spiritual practice can be.

The Power of the Sun

The sun plays an essential role in our existence and is an important symbol in spiritual practices. Frequently used in spiritual visualisations, the sun is seen as a source of light, life, and energy. In addition to providing light, life, and warmth to Earth, the sun also plays an important role in regulating our hormones. Exposure to sunlight during the day decreases melatonin, the sleep hormone, whilst increasing serotonin, a neurotransmitter associated with happiness and well-being production.

Love Lessons:

"As we honor the sun and connect to its energy, we are able to access our own sense of higher knowing."

– JULIA PLEVIN, THE HEALING MAGIC OF FOREST BATHING

Hello, Sun

A monk Plevin met while travelling through Japan shared a practice for connecting with the sun. She advised doing the practice for ten days. If the practice didn't resonate after ten days, it was ok to stop doing it. Plevin has done the practice every day since learning it and advises that it can be done anywhere, at any time of day, although she prefers sunrise:

1. Facing the sun, stand with your arms outstretched in front of you at ninety degrees, with

both palms facing away from you and toward the sun.

2. Bring your thumbs together and place the tips of your four fingers on one hand over the four fingers on the other hand, creating a triangle shape in the space between your hands.

3. Close your eyes and stay still for a moment, feeling the heat of the sun on your palms.

4. Inhale and bring your hands together in prayer position at your heart's centre. Feel the energy of the sun warm your heart.

5. On your next inhale, circle your arms out and bring them back in front of you. Make the same triangle shape with your hands.

6. Repeat this sequence three times or until you feel warmth in your heart. Then, on the last time, hold your hands out in front of you in the same way and say this five-part affirmation, out loud or in silence:

Today is: (the date)

My name is: (your full name)

I am grateful to be born in a human body at this time.

Today I connect to the Universe.

I promise to use my connection as a tool to serve the highest good.

Gently down the stream

My step-mum has always had simple life values. There are few material possessions she places significance on, but she isn't defined or ruled by her possessions. She appreciates nice clothing if it is comfortable, good quality, and the colour suits her. Apart from that, she would say, "the rest can be buggered".

I recall a time when she shared one of her life philosophies with me. She sees our path in life as a river. We are in a boat, and all we can do is sit as comfortably as we can, hang on and enjoy the ride because that boat's goin' down the river. Whether we like it or not, we have no control over it. As a self-confessed control freak, this analogy never sat comfortably with me.

Not *my* boat, I thought. No, *my* boat would have oars … or a rudder, or an outboard motor! Yes, I would be able to steer *my* boat. I wouldn't crash into the banks on either side of the river, and I could navigate around snags and other obstacles. I could never accept that we were that powerless in our own lives, regardless of our destiny. At the very least, I supported Dolly Parton's view: *"We cannot direct the wind, but we can adjust the sails."* Reflecting on this philosophy many years later, I think my stepmother and I may *both* be correct.

The truth is, we don't sail the river alone. The river is crammed with people in all sorts of vessels. Some are in little wooden row boats, being overtaken by flash speedboats and jet-skis, there are yachts, pleasure-cruisers, paddle boards, and even some just wearing life jackets and praying they don't wash up on the bank or get taken out by a bigger vessel. We are all making our own way down the river, in whatever vessel we have been given, in our own time and steering (or not) when necessary. Of course, some are more fortunate than others to be aboard larger, luxurious, faster boats, but the people in the row boats have the opportunity to take in the scenery at a more leisurely pace. This is the way of life.

The one thing we do have on our boats though, is free will. In his book, *Proof of Heaven*, Eben Alexander M.D. attempts to describe the other universes, in addition to ours, that he became aware of during his near-death experience. He writes, "Love lay at the centre of them all. Evil was present in all the other universes as well, but only in the tiniest trace amounts. Evil was necessary because without it free will was impossible, and without free will there could be no growth, no forward movement, no chance for what God longed for us to be."

Although the journey on our vessel can appear predetermined at times, we *always* have choice. The choices presented may not be the ones we want, but nonetheless, there is always another option. Evil may exist, but it serves a very important purpose, and we can take comfort in knowing it is grossly outweighed by Love.

Love Lessons:

1. Think about your boat on the river. What type of vessel are you the captain of, and how do you feel about this? Would you change anything if you could? How can you make your journey down the river as pleasant and scenic as possible?

The Love Bubble

"There is so much love in your heart that you could heal the entire planet. But just for now let us use this love to heal you. Feel a warmth beginning to glow in your heart center, a softness, a gentleness. Let this feeling begin to change the way you think and talk about yourself."

— LOUISE L. HAY,
YOU CAN HEAL YOUR LIFE

Since realising the power of our energy, I've recently started a practice I call The Love Bubble. In *The Spiritual Guidebook: Mastering Psychic Development and Healing Techniques*, Anna Comerford mentions a similar practice she performs called

Ball of Light. She explains: "You imagine a ball of colourful light and place symbols into it. Use whatever symbols, or colours, you feel drawn to ... Ask the ball to travel into your body and send healing to where it needs to go. You can send the healing ball of light to a country, a person or an issue."

My simplified version is imagining a pink ball of loving energy, which I visualise sending out to family and friends who need it. However, I have found the most powerful use of The Love Bubble is on complete strangers. Whenever I encounter someone who looks a bit down, I visualise this ball of loving energy enveloping their whole body, like a force field. With this loving energy, I send positive thoughts and the intention that the difficulties in their life will dissolve, and they will have a great day.

If I walk past them, I often smile and casually make eye contact – without staring them down or making them feel uncomfortable. I expect nothing in return. However, it is amazing the number of occasions people look directly at me or turn around if I am walking behind them, as if they've felt a shift in energy.

If nothing else, this exercise raises *my* energy — especially if I am feeling a bit flat. It shifts the focus from my own problems, makes me feel connected to the world around me, and that I have given someone the ultimate gift — unconditional love.

Home Sweet Home

When we were house-hunting a few years ago, we looked at over a hundred different properties. I love looking at other people's houses; yes, I am a sticky beak. However, I also loved discovering how people lived and interacted within their dwellings.

Throughout the house-hunting process, one thing that struck me was how our emotions are connected to houses — for the buyer *and* the seller. Real-estate agents are all over this, which is why they are eager to get their sellers to invest time and money in decluttering and styling their home for the sales campaign. There is one thing, however, which cannot be removed from a house, and that is 'soul'. If you tune in, the house will share with you what has transpired within her four walls.

After looking at so many houses, I became attuned to which houses had accommodated happy families and memories and which were being sold as the result of relationship breakdown or death. Houses being sold under sad circumstances had a different feeling. Regardless of how beautiful they looked, they smelt and felt different – they had the same quiet melancholy you could imagine settled over Sleeping Beauty's fairy-tale castle as she slept.

I couldn't bring myself to show interest in the houses with this "feeling", which was probably foolish as it narrowed our choices. However, we were planning to live in our prospective house for the next 10+ years, so it had to *feel right*. I often wondered if other buyers picked up on the same vibe I did. Perhaps they did because quite often, these houses would remain on the market for some time before the price was dropped or negotiated down and then finally sold.

After looking at so many houses, there were two things I learnt:

1.   A house can retain the "mood" or "feeling" from its previous occupants.

2.   We have the intuitive ability to sense this.

Of the people who purchased these "sad" houses, I often wonder how they felt after they moved in and if they could shift the negative energy. This is why many people cleanse a new home or space of residual energy by burning white sage or using other cleansing techniques.

The house we eventually purchased and moved into had been renovated with a new kitchen, bathrooms, flooring, and freshly painted. It felt like a blank canvas and was perfect. Some years later, I had the good fortune of meeting the first resident of our house, who had happily raised her family here. Other occupants have come and gone from this house, but I believe it emits a lot of positive energy.

In *The Spiritual Guidebook: Mastering Psychic Development and Healing Techniques*, Anna Comerford writes, "Houses, and buildings, can hold negative or positive energy in them. You may notice a room feels different after an argument or dispute. There are ways to clear and cleanse this energy."

Love lessons:

1. Consider the current energy of your home. It doesn't matter if you are renting at this present moment; it is your space. How do you generally feel in your home? Is it a tranquil sanctuary you look forward to returning to each day? How does it feel at different times of the day, ie does it make you feel energised when you wake up in the morning and relaxed when you wind down in the evening? The feeling I'm referring to is not reserved for specific areas of your home or rooms that require clutter-clearing and cleaning – this is a general feeling.

2. If you feel the energy of your home could be improved, raise the vibration by:

Bringing the outdoors inside by investing in some indoor plants or fresh flowers. Indoor plants are excellent for purifying the air, and the greenery softens the space. Fresh flowers smell great and also add colour, life, and interest to a space. You don't need to buy expensive bunches of flowers, a small sprig of flowers you have growing in your garden, such as lavender or other herbs in a small vase on your bedside table is very uplifting.

Diffuse essential oil blends to calm and soothe or uplift and energise the mood of your home. Comerford suggests spraying essences made from essential oils around your home. These can be made quickly and easily from cooled boiled water mixed with several drops of your favourite essential oils in a spray bottle. The light mist also adds some humidity to the air, which is great for dry climates.

Move your furniture around occasionally. This will make you see your home from a different perspective and might encourage you to use your home differently. For example, moving your loungeroom furniture around might create more floor space for you to stretch or exercise while you are watching TV. Likewise, reorienting your couch might allow you to view and appreciate your garden in a different way. It also allows you to clean properly under larger pieces of furniture and makes your space feel fresher.

3. Let the light in.

"The fact is that very few things have so much effect on the feeling inside a room as the sun shining into it."

— CHRISTOPHER ALEXANDER,
A PATTERN LANGUAGE

We know how important sunlight is for our health, so it stands to reason that light is important within our home too. The simple ritual of throwing open the curtains or blinds each morning marks the start of a new day, as does drawing the curtains when the day comes to an end. Light adds a unique energy to a home, so embrace this as much as possible with the window treatments you select. For example, if you want light as well as privacy, invest in sheer curtains or blinds to preserve privacy whilst filtering light. There is something energising about basking in the winter sun when it streams into your home.

4. Surround yourself with things you love.

This could be photographs of loved ones. I love filling our home with as many of the photos from our yearly family photoshoots as possible. This is one of my favourite family rituals. In years gone by, I would select the best image of the four of us and use this for our Christmas card to family and friends. This image, as well as the other lovely photos included in our package, are all stored away on my computer. For years I regretted not appreciating these more – especially since they were so lovely.

Last year, I finally arranged to get our favourite photo from each year printed on canvas and hung on the dining room wall. The kids have fun reminiscing about themselves at different ages, and they are a great talking point over dinner. Our photographer also takes heart-melting photographs of the kids together, which I like to print and arrange in various frames around the house.

Everyone has special photographs, trinkets and mementos that are often stashed away in draws. These can be tastefully displayed without creating clutter using strategically placed shelves or glass cabinets. Sometimes we become so obsessed with making our home look like a showroom, and we lose sight of the things that make our house a home.

5. Music.

Music can completely transform the feel of a home. I personally love listening to chilled jazz piano. As soon as I hear this type of music, I can instantly feel my muscles relax. I think it is a combination of the slow beat, as well as the delicate piano notes.

One of our favourite purchases has been a portable Bluetooth speaker that is waterproof and can be used outside. I sit it on my desk so I can listen to jazz as I work, or we take it outside to create atmospheric music when we are entertaining. Cleaning also becomes more tolerable with a soundtrack of 80s and 90s power ballads. Not everyone in our household appreciates my music choice – thank goodness for online music streaming apps with specific playlists! Music is one of the quickest and easiest ways to uplift, energise, or relax the mood instantly in your home. What are your favourite types of music to set the mood in your home? How can you listen to music more regularly?

"When you're feeling down, did you know that you can change it in an instant?
Put on a beautiful piece of music, or start singing – that'll change your emotion.

– RHONDA BYRNE, THE SECRET

• CHAPTER 11 •

The Journey Continues …

"In a world of endless questions, love is the only answer."

– MATT KAHN

Infinite Love surrounds us, but sometimes we need to look a little harder or dig a little deeper to connect with it. Love – in its purest form – is free to give, and free to receive. Love connects us to our immediate environment and the people in it: family, friends, work colleagues, and complete strangers. Love is our eternal connection to the world and the Universe. Matt Kahn eloquently captures love's enduring existence in the below passage from his book, *Whatever Arises Love That: A Love Revolution That Begins with You:*

"In every breath you take, love is always here. Throughout any personal encounter, love is always here. No matter what comes together or whatever is pulled apart, love is always here. In your greatest moment of achievement or even in your darkest hour of uncertainty, love is always here. Whether in the aftermath of tragedy or in the presence of your highest triumph, love is always here. When life is flowing, inspired, and harmonious, and even if it's frustrating, annoying, painful, or inconvenient, love is always here. When you feel alone or unsupported, love is always here. No matter what you understand and despite what you have yet to figure out, love is always here. Despite your thoughts, regardless of what you choose, or how you feel, love is always here. No matter what has been done

to you or whatever you believe you've done to others, love is always here."

Throughout my *Year of Love*, new revelations and experiences had a profound impact on my life. Here is my list of the Big-Ticket Items that gave me the greatest "bang for buck" – let's call it a Love Cheat Sheet, if you like. The practice of adding more love to your life is a very personal journey, but these ideas will get you started:

A Year of Love Manifesto

1. Find your 'Flow' by engaging in activities that bring joy to your soul.

2. Identify your personal style and create a style uniform that works for your lifestyle.

3. Fuel your body with high-quality, nutritious food.

4. Establish a sleep routine.

5. Support others to make healthy lifestyle changes.

6. Whistle while you work. Find a job in a field you are passionate about, but accept you will have tough days in any job. If you're not happy at work, change something, or at the very least, the way you think about it.

7. Look for the little opportunities to connect with family every day, such as sharing a meal or a story together, rather than waiting for the weekend or holidays.

8. Nurture existing friendships by exploring creative ways to catch up – it doesn't have to involve an expensive night-out; you can enjoy each other's company by simply going for a walk together.

9. Get to know your neighbours – potential friendships could be right under your nose!

10. At home, make the items you love more accessible so you can use them easily and frequently.

11. Pets are good for the soul – make time to connect with animals.

12. Grow something – in the garden or in a pot on a balcony. There's a plant to fit any space.

13. Spend time in nature – as often as possible.

14. Sit still and quiet, often. Start with two minutes every day, and increase to fifteen minutes (or longer).

15. Remember: *Everyone* deserves to love and be loved.

My hope is for you to reflect on *your* life, and go forth with love!

"Truth is in all, but love is all."

– SRI CHINMOY

ABOUT THE AUTHOR

Courtney Symes is a freelance writer who lives in Canberra, Australia with her husband, two children, Syd the Dog, and six chooks. She loves running along Canberra's spectacular nature trails, Crafternoons, jazz piano, and spending time in her garden. Courtney couldn't survive without books, wine, cheese, and gingernut biscuits. Learn more about Courtney at www.courtneysymes.com.

FREE BONUS: Online Course

Magical Mornings:
The secret to a productive morning routine

If you enjoyed this book, and the content resonated with you, you'll *love* this FREE course.

Magical Mornings is a subject that is very close to my heart and I'm excited to share my learnings and experiences in a course format.

The *Magical Mornings* course will introduce you to a new routine that will have you jumping out of bed with new-found energy and a zest for life EVERY DAY.

The content in this course has been created from over 15 years of tried, tested, and PROVEN learnings and techniques – this is my "magic bullet" for juggling family, work, exercise, personal development, and everything in between.

By using this routine, I have:
- ✅ Created four different businesses
- ✅ Written a book
- ✅ Completed courses and excelled my learning by consuming hundreds of online tutorials and videos
- ✅ Practiced piano
- ✅ Established a regular meditation practice
- ✅ Exercised and run hundreds of kilometres and more...

Magical Mornings will teach you how to:
- ✧ Create a Magical Morning routine that resonates with your life RIGHT NOW.
- ✧ Define what is important in your life and how you can create a Magical Morning to achieve this.
- ✧ Implement powerful self-care rituals to promote physical activity, personal development and learning, spirituality, connection with others, and organisation for the day ahead.

✺ Set yourself up for the day with intention, clarity and focus so you can tackle whatever comes your way with calm confidence – all before 7am! It's COMPLETELY FREE! I'd love for you to check it out at www.pinkplatform.thinkific.com.

Suggestions for further reading

Books:

Alcott, Louisa May, 2012, *Little Women*, Random House, London

Alexander, Eben, 2012, *Proof of Heaven: A Neurosurgeon's Journey into the Afterlife*, Simon & Schuster, New York

Baird, Julia, *Phosphorescence: On Awe, Wonder And Things That Sustain You When The World Goes Dark*, 2020, HarperCollins, Australia

Barrie, J. M., 2015, *Peter Pan*, HarperCollins, United States

Benzakein, Erin, 2017, *Floret Farm's Cut Flower Garden: Grow, Harvest, and Arrange Stunning Seasonal Blooms*, Chronicle Books, United States

Bond, Michael, 2018, *Paddington Turns Detective and Other Funny Stories*, HarperCollins Children's Books, London

Burchard, Brendon, 2017, *High Performance Habits: How Extraordinary People Become That Way*, Hay House, California

Byrne, Rhonda, 2013, *Hero*, Atria Books, New York

Carle, Eric, 2011, *The Very Hungry Caterpillar*, Puffin Books, London

Comerford, Anna, 2018, *The Spiritual Guidebook*, Rockpool Publishing, Summer Hill, NSW

Csikszentmihalyi, Mihaly, 2008, *Flow: The Psychology of Optimal Experience*, Harper Perennial Modern Classics, New York

Dahl, Roald, 2017, *Matilda,* Puffin, United States

Dunn, Cassandra, 2019, *Crappy to Happy: Love What You Do,* Hardie Grant Books, Australia

Dyer, Wayne, 2019, *Happiness is the Way: How to Reframe Your Thinking and Work with What You Already Have to Live the Life of Your Dreams*, Hay House, California

Gilbert, Elizabeth, 2016, *Big Magic: Creative Living Beyond Fear*, Bloomsbury, Great Britain

Harris, Michael, 2018, *Solitude*, Random House, London

Haskell, David George, 2017, *The Songs Of Trees: Stories from Nature's Great Connectors*, Viking

Herz, Rachel, 2008, *The Scent of Desire: Discovering Our Enigmatic Sense of Smell*, HarperCollins, United States

Hodgson Burnett, Frances, 2018, *The Secret Garden*, HarperCollins, United States

Kahn, Matt, 2016, *Whatever Arises, Love That: A Love Revolution That Begins with You*, Sounds True, Colorado

Lewis, C.S., 2015, *The Chronicles of Narnia*, HarperCollins, London

McConnell, Patricia, 2003, *The Other End of the Leash*, Ballantine Books, New York

Michalewicz, Matthew, 2013, *Life in Half a Second*, Hybrid Publishers Pty Ltd, Australia

Montgomery, Lucy Maud, 1993, *Anne of Green Gables*, Random House, United States

Plevin, Julia, 2019, *The Healing Magic of Forest Bathing*, Ten Speed Press, United States

Robbins, Mel, *The 5 Second Rule: Transform Your Life, Work, and Confidence with Everyday Courage*, Permuted Press, United States

Rowling, J.K., 2014, *Harry Potter and the Philosopher's Stone*, Bloomsbury, London

Rubin, Gretchen, 2011, *The Happiness Project: Or Why I Spent a Year Trying to Sing in the Morning, Clean My Closets, Fight Right, Read Aristotle, and Generally Have More Fun*, Harper, New York

Seligman, Martin E. P., *Flourish: A New Understanding of Happiness and Well-Being - and How to Achieve Them*, 2011, Nicholas Brealey, London

Sisson, Mark, 2017, *The Keto Reset Diet: Reboot your metabolism in 21 days and burn fat forever*, Harmony Books, United States

Stephenson, Lisa, 2018, *Read Me First Before you write the next chapter in the story of you*, Major Street Publishing Pty Ltd, Australia

Walsch, Neale Donald, 1996, *Conversations with God: An Uncommon Dialogue, Book 1*, G.P. Putnam's Sons, New York

Williams, Florence, 2018, *The Nature Fix: Why Nature Makes Us Happier, Healthier, and More Creative*, WW Norton and Company, United States

Williamson, Marianne, 2007, *A Return to Love: Reflections on the Principles of "A Course in Miracles*, HarperCollins, United States

Wiking, Meik, 2016, *The Little Book of Hygge: The Danish Way to Live Well*, Penguin, London

Huffington, Arianna, 2017, *The Sleep Revolution: Transforming Your Life, One Night at a Time*, Harmony, United States

Podcasts:

Burchard, Brendon (Host), 2014-present, How to Assess Opportunities (ep. 106) [Audio podcast episode] in The Brendon Show, The Burchard Group

Articles:

Li, Qing, 2018, 'Forest Bathing' Is Great for Your Health. Here's How to Do It', Time, 1 May, accessed26/11/2020, <https://time.com/5259602/japanese-forest-bathing/>

Notes

www.ingramcontent.com/pod-product-compliance
Lightning Source LLC
Chambersburg PA
CBHW071955290426
44109CB00018B/2026